Other books by Cynthia Farrar Burse available from your local bookstore:

For the Record: The Testimonies of Mary Magdalene and Judas Iscariot

A Little Bible Dictionary for

Believers, Seekers and Other Spirit Chasers

Cynthia Farrar Burse

A Little Bible Dictionary for Believers, Seekers and Other Spirit Chasers

Copyright © 2025 by Cynthia F. Burse. All rights reserved.

Paperback: ISBN 979-8-9923986-1-8

Library of Congress Control Number: 2025906731

Cover Image: Canva. Used by permission.

Cover Design: Cynthia Farrar Burse

The contents of this book are protected by U.S. Copyright laws. Reproduction of this material without written permission of the author or credit assigned to the author is prohibited.

To request permission, contact the publisher at: resilience976@gmail.com

Exact scripture quotations are taken from the ESV® Bible (The Holy Bible, English Standard Version®), copyright © 2001 by Crossway, a publishing ministry of Good News Publishers. Used by permission. All rights reserved.

Printed by Ingram Spark, TN

Published by Cynthia Farrar Burse, Columbus, OH

This book is consecrated to that great multitude coming out of every peoples, tribes, languages and nations, and the twelve tribes of Israel.

Introduction

The Bible has an influence over my life that's different from any other important book I've ever read, and from the many conversations I've had as a congregational pastor (now retired), I know I'm not alone in thinking this way.

The function of this little Bible dictionary is to serve as a resource for Believers who are studying to show themselves approved, as an orderly presentation to help make sense of the Bible for those in seeking-mode, and as a guide to help and encourage other spirit chasers in the world.

To engage the book, simply think of a word you know is in the Bible or that you've often wondered about and search for it in the dictionary. If you don't find it in this edition, choose another word. Rinse and repeat until you come across a defined word that calls to you and follow it down the rabbit hole.

If you have ever wanted to know who GOD is, what it means to be a child of GOD, and why GOD is justified in doing whatever GOD does, this book is for you.

And please write to me at resilience976@gmail.com to let me know what word(s) you'd like to see added to the next edition, because my purpose in this life is to help lessen the distance between GOD, the academy, the church pew and the back alley, one word at a time.

2 Timothy 2:5-7

Abel (see Cain and Abel)

Abide in Me

> To take refuge in the LORD; 2. Akin to "Marry me, choose me."; 3. The opposite of hooking up on social media for a one-night stand in a stranger's bed, an expensive suite, or the nearest Motel 6.
>
> (Psalm 91:1-10; John 15:1-11; 1 John 2:4-6, 28-29, 3:24; Revelation 3:20)

Abomination

> The devious and arrogant in heart; 2. Unclean, irreverent, detestable or false.
>
> (Genesis 43:32, 46:34; Leviticus 11:10-13, 13:14-15; Deuteronomy 17:1, 25:16; Proverbs 3:32, 6:16, 11:1, 20, 12:22, 15:8, 9, 26, 16:5, 17:15, 20:10, 21:27, 26:24-25, etc.; Isaiah 1:13-14, 44:9-10, 18-19; Revelation 21:22, 27)

Abraham

> The man of faith and father of many nations.
>
> (Genesis 12:1-4, 15:1-6, 16:1-4, 15-16, 17:1-23, 21:1-7, 22:1-18; Hebrews 11:8, 17-18)

Abundance

> Having and receiving nothing less than everything one needs; 2. Something more being added to what has already been given, said or done, pressed down, shaken together and running over.
>
> (Deuteronomy 28:1-14; Psalm 23:5, 37:11; Matthew 6:33, 13:12; John 10:10; 2 Corinthians 9:8; Ephesians 3:20; Philippians 4:19)

Accountability

> The duty to hold one's self responsible for achieving agreed upon measurable outcomes and be mature enough to voluntarily explain the failure to do so.
>
> (Romans 14:10-12; 2 Corinthians 5:10)

Advent

> An arrival, appearing or coming; 2. The seasonal church tradition celebrating Jesus of Nazareth's first advent into the world as a baby, coupled with biblical exhortations and reminders to keep watch for His second arrival/appearing/coming as King.
>
> (Isaiah 40:10, Daniel 7:13; Malachi 3:1-2a; Matthew 25:1-13, 26:64; Mark 1:1-3, 13:32-37, 14:62; Luke 2:4-7, 21, 12:35-40, 21:28; John 1:6-9, 14-18; Revelation 1:7, 14:14, 22:12-13)

Adversary

> Someone who clearly opposes another; 2. One who outwardly offers or states support for a goal while holding personal views and agendas in direct opposition to that goal.
>
> (Exodus 23:22; Judges 16:15-19; 1 Kings 11:14, 13:11-18; Esther 5:9-14; Revelation 13:11)

Angel (Gabriel)

> A mighty heavenly warrior angel.
>
> (Daniel 9:20-23; 10:5-6, 13-14)

Angel (Michael)

> The great Prince who has charge over Daniel, his people (Israel), and all the heavenly hosts.
>
> (Daniel 8:11, 10:13, 12:1-3; 1 Thessalonians 4:16; Jude 1:9; Revelation 12:7-8)

Angels

> Divine celestial guardians, servants and messengers of GOD, each having specific authorities and assigned duties (guardians of holy spaces, temple worship, warrior and ministering angels, authority over the elements of nature, etc.); 2. The unholy celestial guardians, servants and messengers of Satan; 3. The term occasionally refers to a human servant or messenger.
>
> (Genesis 3:24, 19:1, 28:10-12; Exodus 23:20-21; Numbers 22:22; 1 Kings 23-28; Psalm 91:11; Ezekiel 1:4-14, 10:5-8, 41:18-20; Daniel

8:16, 9:21; Matthew 2:19-20, 4:11, 13:41,18:10, 24:31, 26:53-54; Luke 9:51-52; 2 Corinthians 12:7; James 2:25; Hebrews 1:4-5; Jude 1:6; Revelation 4:6b-8, 7:1-3, 11, 19:9-10, 22:8-9)

Antichrist (The)

Also known as Hasatan, the Dragon, Satan, the Devil, and the Serpent. After being defeated in battle, the Antichrist is thrown into the lake of fire and sulfur; 2. The enemy of Jesus and the righteous offspring who keep the commandments of GOD and hold to the testimony of Jesus; 3. A created-being exalting itself as GOD; 4. The one through whom all other antichrists come, whereby evil, hatred, deceit and violence are replicated and passed on through the serpent's seed or offspring. Its fury is particularly directed against those refusing to compromise GOD's commandments or the testimony of Jesus.

(Genesis 3:1-15; Job 1:6-12, 2:1-6; John 8:44; 1 John 2:22-23; 2 John 1:7; Revelation 12:1-6, 17a, 20:1-10)

Apocrypha

Meaning hidden or secret things. The term ordinarily refers to fourteen specific books of ancient Jewish and Christian literature that exist outside the canonical, or authorized, Bible.

(1 Edras; 2 Edras; Tobit; Judith; Additions to Esther; Wisdom of Solomon; Ecclesiastes (Sirach); Baruch; Letter of Jeremiah; 1 Maccabees; 2 Maccabees; Susanna; Bel and the Dragon; Prayer of Manesseh)

Asleep

The state of unconsciousness or unpreparedness; 2. Sleeping in death; 3. Truth and fact are unremembered, unrecognized, ignored, or rejected by the conscious mind.

(Isaiah 6:9-10; Matthew 25:5; Mark 14:37; 1 Thessalonians 4:13-15; Revelation 3:1-3)

Assimilate

> To blend into the status quo so smoothly that one is indistinguishable from it and emotionally incapable of standing outside it.
>
> (John 12:42-43)

Assyria

> Land of the Assyrians, where king Sennacherib was allowed by GOD to take the northern kingdom of Israel into captivity because of their disobedience. This group was later called the <u>ten lost tribes of Israel</u>. GOD's promise was to bring the lost sheep bring back to Jerusalem (the nation of Israel was reestablished in 1948).
>
> (Genesis 10:6-11, 2 Kings 17:6-13, 18:13-16, 19:20, 32-37; Isaiah 1:1-31, 10:5-6, 11:10-16, 19:23-25, 27:12-13, 36:1; Jeremiah 30:1-3, 31:10; Hosea 11:5; Amos 3:1-2, 9:9-10; Matthew 10:5-7, 15:21-24)

Baal

> A term or name representing a false god or idol being worshiped as lord.
>
> (Numbers 25:1-3; Deuteronomy 4:1-3; Joshua 11:16-17: Judges 8:33-34; 1 Samuel 7:3-4; 1 Kings 16:30-31, 18:17-19, 22, 25-29, 40; 2 Kings 1:2-3, 10:18-23; 1 Chronicles 5:5, 8:30; Jeremiah 2:8, 19:4-5, 23:13; Hosea 13:1; Zephaniah 1:4-6)

Babylon

> The land of the Chaldeans, where a number of people from the southern kingdom of Judah were deported by GOD's vassal, king Nebuchadnezzar (597 BCE), because of Israel's disobedience and rebellion against GOD. The king of Judah (Jehoiakim) was captured and his son was appointed king by Nebuchadnezzar. A second deportation took place in 587 BCE, and Jerusalem and the temple were destroyed. In 582 BCE, a third deportation took place after Gedaliah, the Babylonian governor appointed by Nebuchadnezzar, was assassinated.

(Genesis 10:8-10, 11:1-9; 2 Kings 24:1; 1 Chronicles 9:1; 2 Chronicles 36:5-21; Psalm 137:8; Isaiah 13:1-13, 47, 21:9; Jeremiah 21:1-2, 24-25:14, 29:10, 50:1-51:64; Daniel 2:1-49, 3:1-7)

Babylon (The Great)

The great city; 2. A dwelling place for demons; 3. The name written on the forehead of the great prostitute; 4. Mother of prostitutes and of earth's atrocities (abominations).

(Revelation 14:8, 16:17-17:5, 18:1-24)

Balaam

A term calling to mind one who is a seducer or devourer of people; 2. The son of Beor; 3. The non-Israelite prophet-for-hire who disobeyed GOD and taught Balak, king of Moab, how to weaken the Israelites by enticing them to commit sin using idol worship and sexual immorality.

(Number 22:1-6, 22, 24:3, 25:1-9, 31:1-9, 16; Micah 6:5; 2 Peter 2:15-16; Jude 1:11; Revelation 2:14)

Baptism

Christian church sacrament or ritual where one is sprinkled with water, or briefly submerged under water, as a visible symbol of having been born again by water and the spirit; 2. To be made spiritually clean and received as a child of GOD in the name of the Father, Son and Holy Spirit; 3. A public demonstration of one's commitment to and faith in Jesus; 4. In Jewish tradition and in fulfillment of Jewish Law, the baptismal purification ritual is referred to as *mikveh* ([Matthew 3:13-15). In Islam, the purity ritual is called *taharah*.

(Exodus 19:10-11; Leviticus 8:6, 14:8-9; Matthew 28:19; Mark 1:9-11; John 1:29-34, 3:3,5; Acts 10:47-48)

Be Still

To wait patiently for the Lord and fret not; 2. To be silent, stand firm, hold one's position, and see the salvation of the Lord on one's behalf; 3. To stop for a moment and consider the wondrous works of GOD.

(Exodus 14:14; 2 Chronicles 20:17; Psalm 37:7, 46:10; Isaiah 40:31: Revelation 6:9-11)

Beast (The Great Scarlet)

The animal/physical embodiment of the great antichrist, having seven heads and ten horns; 2. A political or religious demon who appears during the final phase of GOD's divine plan to finish dismantling all empires on earth, and establish justice and peace throughout the created order; 3. Created in the image of the dragon who once stood on the sandy floor of the sea; 4. The Beast who was and is not; 5. Wild, untamed and dangerous.

The great beast rises from the bottomless pit. It is covered with blasphemous names, has seven heads and ten horns, and is in alliance with the great prostitute. The seven heads are seven kings, or rulers. At the time John sees this vision, five of the rulers have perished, one is currently ruling, and the seventh is still to come, but will rule only a short time.

(Daniel 7:7-8; Revelation 11:7, 12:17b, 17:3, 7-17; 20:7-10; Mark 1:12-13)

Beast (The First)

Son of the Hasatan/Satan/Dragon/Devil/Great (scarlet) Beast; 2. The lawless one/the man of lawlessness; 3. The little horn; 4. The eighth beast that was and is not, which belongs to the seven and goes to destruction.

(Revelation 13:1-8, 18, 17:7-14, 20:10; Daniel 7:8; 2 Thessalonians 2:1-12)

- This first beast is created in the image and likeness of the Great Beast. It has ten horns and seven heads and rises out of the sea (the sand of the sea[floor] where the dragon previously stood). On each horn (representing ten rulers) is a diadem, or crown, signifying that the power, throne and authority of the Dragon/Great Beast has been transferred to the first beast, making them one and of one mind. Written on each of the seven heads (signifying kings) is language which is profane, indecent, immoral, disrespectful and, abusive (Revelation 13:1).

- The beast is savage and monstrous in both appearance and behavior, and is a cross-breed of the four beasts (lion, eagle, bear and leopard) spoken of by Daniel, but more terrifying than them all. The beast is offensive, spiteful and vicious, with a loud blasphemous and boasting mouth. It seeks to eliminate, destroy and overpower the principled and ethical, and to subjugate and suppress different cultures, peoples, nations and races. It receives a potentially deadly wound but does not die. Many people of the Earth admire the creature, as though the whole world was following it, guided by their false belief the beast is invincible. Those who marvel after the beast are among those whose names have not been written in the book of life. (Daniel 7:3-7; Revelation 13:2-8).
- The beast is identified by the number 666 rather than a name (some fragments of the earliest scripture manuscripts record the number as 616). Scholars have typically responded to the invitation to calculate the number of the beast using a process called gematria, a Hebraic numerological system. The process decodes the numerical value of a word or name by adding together the numerical values associated with each Hebrew letter (i.e. *beit*, second letter of the Hebrew alphabet, has a numerical value of 2. *Shin*, next-to-last alphabet letter, has a value of 300). With the help of gematria, many men have been identified as the first beast, or as the Antichrist (i.e. Nero, Martin Luther, several catholic popes, etc.) (Revelation 13:18).
- A case can be made for also including names of more contemporary figures, using simpler methods. Ronald Wilson Reagan, 40th president of the United States who survived a March 30, 1981 assassination attempt on his life, had six letters in each of his names (666). Similarly, Donald J. Trump, 45th and 47th President of the United States, is the former owner and resident of 666 Trump Tower (officially 666 Fifth Avenue). The property was later re-numbered 660 Fifth Avenue. Trump also survived an assassination attempt when a bullet grazed his ear during a July 13, 2024 campaign rally, missing a direct hit to his head by fractions of an inch. Also noteworthy is the nickname of the presidential limousine, "The Beast".

- The combination of a beast with ten horns and seven heads, the New Testament reports of there being many antichrists in the world, and Daniel's vision of four beasts seem to support the idea of there being many beasts throughout history. This may be why each generation since the time of Jesus has had the right, and the right reasons, to suppose the end was near. In Luke 21:29-33, using a parable, Jesus clarifies how to distinguish between the times of the end (i.e. Time, Times, and half a Time). The question one is to consider is, "What do you see?" (Jeremiah 1:11-16; Ezekiel 37:1-3; Matthew 24:1-51; Mark 13:1-37; Luke 21:20-28).

Second Beast

The False Prophet.

(Revelation 13:11-17, 16:13, 19:19-20, 20:10; Deuteronomy 13:1-1-5, 18:20-22; Jeremiah 5:30-31, 14:14, 23:16-20; Ezekiel 13:9; Matthew 7:15-20, 24:24-25; Mark 13:22-23; Luke 6:26; Romans 16:17-18; 2 Corinthians 11:13-15)

- The beast rises out of the Earth, appearing as one who looks like a Believer but is not. Its speech is like that of the Great Dragon (Hasatan/Satan who attempted to overthrow GOD's throne). A symbiotic relationship exists between the first and second beast. The second beast can only exercise its authority with the approval and direction of the first, and the first beast is seemingly dependent on the second to implement its agenda and maintain control over the people of Earth (Revelation 13:11-12).
- The second beast is given the ability to accomplish great signs and wondrous works, by which it is able to deceive the people of Earth. As Aaron built the golden calf, the beast commands a likeness be built of the (first) beast that was wounded and lived. The image and likeness of the first beast is given movement and speech (using artificial intelligence?), and it declares that those who will not worship it are to be killed. The second beast issues a command that all persons—small, great, rich and poor—must pledge allegiance to the empire's god (the first beast). Each person must be marked on their right hand or

forehead with either the name of the beast, or the number of its name. Those refusing to do so lose the right to buy and sell (i.e. food, medicine, etc.). The second beast is the third member of the unholy trinity comprised of the dragon, the beast and the false prophet (Revelation 12:9, 13:12-17, 16:13-14; Exodus 32:1-30; Daniel 3:1-7).

Behold

Code word for "Look, listen, and pay attention", toward the goal of becoming wise or having some matter confirmed.

(Isaiah 7:14, 43:19; Luke 1:26-33, 2:1-21; John 1:29; Revelation 21:3-5, 22:12)

Belief System

An ideology or thought system of principles, ideas and assumptions that are founded or established on either the Spirit of Truth or the spirit of error.

(Genesis 3:4-5, 13; Psalm 121:1; Daniel 1:12-14; Acts 11:1-4, 18; 1 Thessalonians 4:1-12; 1 John 4:1-6)

Believer

One who confesses Jesus (Yeshua) of Nazareth as Savior and Lord, obeys the commands of GOD and the Lord Jesus by doing what they say to do, and endures to the end; 2. One whose faith does not continually waver and doubt.

(Matthew 7:24-25, 10:22, 16:24; Mark 16:16; Luke 6:46-48; John 3:16, 9:31, 12:26; 14:12-14; 2 Corinthians 6:14-7:1; 2 Timothy 2:24-26; Hebrews 11:6; 1 Peter 3:13-17)

Bible

The sacred book of Judaism and Christianity. For Judaism, the Bible consists of the Hebrew Bible (aka Old Testament). For Christianity, it refers to the Hebrew Bible together with the New Testament (with or without the Apocrypha); 2. A bound assortment of inspired, sometimes competing, theological belief systems; 3. A teaching device explaining GOD's will, ways, plans and interest in behavior over professed belief, and the "if you…then I will" conditional nature of GOD's promises, using words as symbols of symbols to guide people into an awareness of GOD's love and presence.

(Isaiah 42:9; 2 Timothy 3:14-17)

Blameless

To walk in the law and way of the Lord and do no wrong.

(Psalm 119:1-3)

Blessing

A gift given in true generosity of spirit for the well-being of the receiver.

(Genesis 2:2-3, 49:28; Exodus 20:8-11; Mark 2:27-28; Luke 7:37-38; John 5:5-6; Romans 12:6-8; 2 Corinthians 9:10-11)

Blindness

To look but not see with one's eyes and/or understand in one's spirit and heart.

(Isaiah 42:16; John 9:1-7, 13-15, 18, 24-25, 34-41; Acts 9:8-9; 1 Corinthians 2:14)

Cain and Abel

The first two sons born of the union between the first Woman and Man. Some resources suggest the brothers were twins—the Bible is not clear on the matter—but Cain is clearly identified as the older of the two. He grows up to become a farmer while Abel becomes a shepherd, a keeper of sheep. Cain becomes angry, perhaps even feels hurt, when GOD accepts an offering from Abel but will not accept Cain's offering. In the opinion of GOD, Cain's gift is polluted in some way. Being unable to hold hands with sin, GOD cannot accept anything from Cain's hand. In revenge, Cain takes his brother Abel to a field and murders him. Instead of retaliating in kind, GOD puts a mark of protection on Cain and sends him away; 2. Abel is the first righteous son of GOD to die by the hand of violence. Cain is the father of those Jesus held responsible for spilling the righteous blood of the prophets and innocent people like Abel and Zechariah.

(Genesis 4:1-26; Malachi 1:10; Matthew 23:29-36; John 8:39-47; Hebrews 11:4)

Capitalism

> Out-buying and out-selling one's neighbor with no thought for their survival.
>
> (Exodus 22:25-27; Leviticus 19:13, 25:35-37; Amos 8:4-6; Matthew 19:23-24, 20:8-16; Philippians 2:3-4)

Chaldeans

> An aggressive and warlike people belonging to Babylonian culture.
>
> (Isaiah 13:19, 47:1, 5, 48:14; Daniel 5:7, 9:1-2; Luke 12:4-5; Acts 7:2-7; Revelation 18:1-3)

Child (in the Spirit)

> Unskilled in the ways and words of GOD and righteousness; 2. Toddler milk drinkers.
>
> (John 16:12; Hebrews 5:11-14)

Child/Children of GOD

> Individuals who come out of all the world's nations, tribes, peoples, tongues and all twelve tribes of Israel, who know and do the will of GOD. Under GOD's new Covenant with Noah and all flesh on the earth, Israel no longer constitutes the only children of GOD. Faith and belief in Yeshua/Jesus as the promised Deliverer of Israel is decreed sufficient to justify Gentiles also as children of GOD.
>
> (Genesis 9:1-17; Isaiah 56:6-8; Matthew 12:46-50; Mark 3:11-12; Luke 22:66-71; John 1:11-13, 49, 3:16-18, 5:18, 23, 10:14-15, 34-38, 17:1-5, 20:30-31; Romans 8:14; 2 Corinthians 6:17-18; Galatians 3:23-29; Ephesians 2:11-22; Philippians 2:14-15; Hebrews 2:14-18; 1 Peter 2:7-10; 2 Peter 1:1-11; 1 John 3:1-3, 4:15; Revelation 7:9-10)

Children of Israel

> Covering the generational tribal offspring of Abram/Abraham, his second born son Isaac, and his grandson Jacob, whose name was later

changed to Israel. Not by GOD, but by a man on the losing end of a wrestling match with Jacob. When Jacob insists the man bless him, he is told that his name will no longer be Jacob, but Israel, because by prevailing over the man in the sparring match, Jacob had prevailed over GOD. Is the man claiming to be GOD? When Jacob asks the man his name, he does not answer, but gives him the blessing he requested instead. Jacob believes he has seen GOD face to face. The principle difficulty with this tradition is that no man is powerful enough to prevail over or against GOD. The second problem is how similar the man's words sounds to what the serpent said to the woman in the garden: "You will not die...you will be like GOD..."; 2. Abraham's sons in order of birth: Ishmael, whose mother was an Egyptian servant named Hagar; Isaac, whose mother was Sarai/Sarah; Zimran, Jokshan, Medan, Midian, Ishbak and Shuah, whose mother was Keturah.

(Genesis 3:1-5; 16:1-17:8, [the New Covenant has succeeded the Old Covenant],17:15-21, 25:1-18, 32:22-30; 1 Chronicles 1:28-36, 29:10-11; Ezra 3:1)

Children of This World

Deniers of GOD and Truth from whom life has removed all innocence; 2. Shrewd, wicked people who do not tremble before the Lord.

(Luke 16:8; John 8:39-47; Ephesians 2:1-2; 1 John 2:22-23, 3:1b, 10)

Chosen/Called

Individuals and spirits on whom GOD's divine favor settles and remains who are placed into service for specific purposes according to GOD's plans; 2. A belief system which says that while GOD's character and willful intent is always to do good to others, GOD grants certain kindnesses, advantages and benefits to some but not to others, specifically to those who obey; 3. Called by and faithful to GOD.

(Deuteronomy 7:6, 14:2; 1 Kings 22:20-23; Psalm 31:19-20, 145:9; Isaiah 43:10, 61:9; Jeremiah 1:4-5, 29:11; Matthew 5:44-45, 11:27, 22:13-14; John 6:44, 15:16; Romans 8:28-30; Colossians James 1:16-18; 1 Peter 2:9)

Christ (The)

> Title given to Yeshua/Jesus of Nazareth that distinguishes between His divine personhood as LORD, Savior and Head of the church from His human, earthly personhood.
>
> (Isaiah 53; Micah 5:2; Matthew 24:4-5, 27:22; John 8:58; Acts 1:6-11, 2:38; Romans 6:4, 11, 23; 1 Corinthians 8:5-6, 12:27; Galatians 2:15-21; Philippians 3;20-21; Colossians 1:15-19; 1 Timothy 2:5-6; Hebrews 12:2; 1 John 5:20; Revelation 1:1a).

Christian

> A term first adopted by a community of Jesus-followers in the city of Antioch under the leadership of disciples Barnabas and Paul. Prior to the term coming into existence and being used, followers of Jesus were referred to as people of the *Way*.
>
> (Acts 9:1-2, 11:25-26)

Command/Commandment

> The WORD that shall be done; 2. An unconditional and/or direct order or instruction, teaching, ruling, requirement, law, imperative, or decree; 3. Rules designed to help and not harm.
>
> (Exodus 20:1-17; Leviticus 19: Deuteronomy 6:5-6; Job 36:10-12; Matthew 5:17-20; Luke 10:25-28; John 13:34-35, 14:15; Romans 1:32; 1 Corinthians 7:17; Galatians 5:14-15; James 2:8-13; Psalm 119:166)

Compassion

> Acts of grace and mercy.
>
> (Exodus 22:27b, 33:17-19; Psalm 78:38, 103:13; Mark 6:34; Luke 6:36; Acts 28:2; Galatians 6:2; Ephesians 4:32; Colossians 3:12-13; James 5:11; 1 Peter 4:10; 1 John 3:17-18)

Confidence

> The assuredness felt by the saints and children of GOD even as the world shakes in fear.

(Joshua 1:9; Psalm 91:1-16, 138:8; Proverbs 29:25, 14:26; Isaiah 41:10, 13; Jeremiah 17:7; Matthew 26:53; John 3:16; Hebrews 4:16, 10:35-36, 13:6; James 1:12; 1 John 2:28-3:1; 5:14)

Contentment

> To live with a quiet mind regarding present conditions and how much one currently has.
>
> (Psalm 23:1, 37:7, 16; Proverbs 3:5-6, 16:8, 19:23, 28:6, 30:8-9; Ecclesiastes 4:6: Habakkuk 3:17-18; Philippians 4:11-12)

Court

> A system or an instrument used to reach and administer judgment.
>
> (Judges 4:4-5; Daniel 7:10; John 18:19-24, 28-31; Revelation 20:11-15)

Covenant (The New/Eternal)

> An oath; 2. A promise; 3. The handshake of faithfulness.
>
> (Psalm 111:1-10; Isaiah 55:1-3, 61:8-9; Jeremiah 31:31-34, 33:24-26, 50:4-7; Ezekiel 37:15-28; Matthew 5:33-37; Mark 14:22-24; Romans 9:1-26; Hebrews 6:13-20; 8: 1-13, 12:18-29, 13:20-21)

Covenant (Old/Former)

> An oath; 2. A promise; 3. The handshake of faithfulness.
>
> (Genesis 2:23-25, 9: 8-17, 17:1; 28:10-22, 31:44-50; Exodus 6:2-9, 24:1-8 (v. 9-18 is a different version of this covenant story), 31:16-17; Leviticus 26:3-13; Joshua 9:16-20, 24:14-27; Judges 2:1-3; 1 Samuel 18:1-5; 2 Samuel 15:7-9; 2 Chronicles 15:12-17; Psalm 89:20-36, 105:3-11, 106:1-48; Isaiah 59:1-4, 8-9; Ezekiel 16:59-63, 17:16-19; Jeremiah 11:1-8, 33:19-22, 35:1-19; Daniel 9:2427; Malachi; 2:1-9; Matthew 5:1-39, 23:16-22; Hebrews 6:9:1-28)

Critical Thinker

> One who studies a matter, asks effective questions and demonstrates an understanding and mastery of a discipline or point-at-issue
>
> (Ezra 7:10; Luke 2:46-47; 2 Timothy 2:15)

Cross

> A religious symbol of the Christian faith; 2. The tool used to crucify Yeshua/Jesus of Nazareth, and ancient Rome's execution instrument of choice.
>
> (Luke 23:26, 33; John 19:16-18)

Crossroad

> The moment when one must decide, because things just can't go on as they have been.
>
> (Joshua 24:14-15; Isaiah 30:21; Jeremiah 6:16; Acts 15:36-40)

Darkness

> A state of spiritual blindness or ignorance; 2. What remains when light is absent in the world; 3. That which separates a person from being aware of Love's (GOD's) presence; 4. Nighttime, when beasts creep about.
>
> (Genesis 1:1-5; Psalms 104:20, 139:11-12; Proverbs 4:19; Ecclesiastes 2:13; Micah 7:8; John 12:35c; Romans 1:21, 28, 32)

Day of the Lord (see Coming of the Lord)

Death (First)

> The termination of vital signs (breathing, heartbeat, blood pressure, consciousness, temperature); 2. The separation of the soul/spirit from the physical body and visible world; 3. Entering into restful sleep; 4. A component of GOD's rescue plan.
>
> (Psalm 23:4, 115:17, 116:15, 146:4; Ecclesiastes 9:5; Isaiah 25:8, 57:1-2; Matthew 10:28; Mark 5:35-42; John 11:25; Romans 8:38-39; 1 Corinthians 15:12-26, 50-55; Philippians 1:21; Hebrews 2:14-16, 9:27; Revelation 1:17-18, 9:6, 12:11, 14:13, 20:14-15)

Death (Second)

> Eternal death away from the presence of GOD; 2. The lake of fire.
>
> (Daniel 12:2; Matthew 10:26-28, 25:41-46; 2 Thessalonians 1:9; Hebrews 9:27; Revelation 2:11, 20:6, 10, 14-15, 21:8)

Declares the Lord

>GOD's testimony as communicated in WORD according to the Prophets.

>(1 Kings 22:14; Jeremiah 23:16a, 23-32, 29:11, 31:31; 2 Peter 1:21)

Deeds

>The actions and behaviors performed by a person; 2. What one actually does (works) over what one says they intend to do (words); 3. Doers of the word and not hearers only.

>(Psalm 119:1-8; Proverbs 14:23; Jonah 3:10; Matthew 7:21, 12:36-37, 21:28-31b; Romans 12:6-8; 1 Corinthians 16:13-14; James 1:19-25; 1 John 3:18; Revelation 2:2, 19, 3:1b, c, 8, 15)

Deliverer

>One who intervenes to save.

>(Judges 3: 9,15a; 2 Samuel 22:2-4; Ezekiel 37:5—6; Psalm 18:2, 40:17; Matthew 16:27; Luke 19:10; John 3:16-17, 6:50-51; Romans 11:26-27; Galatians 5:1; Philippians 2:10-11; Revelation 17:14)

Discernment

>Spiritual knowledge and wisdom; 2. The ability to judge well based on what actually is or how things actually are; 3. The ability to see what is not readily evident or apparent to others; 4. The spiritual ability to recognize truth from error; 5. To catch sight of the wisdom that GOD speaks; 6. Prudence and common sense; 7. One who finds knowledge and understands.

>(2 Samuel 14:1; 1 Kings 3:9, 22:19-23; 2 Kings 4: 9; Proverbs 8:5-9, 15:14, 18:15; Matthew 10:16; John 4:19, 7:24; Romans 12:2; 1 Corinthians 2:14; Ephesians 5:6-10; Philippians 1:9-11; Hebrews 4: 12, 5:11-14; James 1:5, 3:13-18; 1 John 4:1)

Disciple

>One who is a student of another.

>(Acts 9:1-2)

Double-minded

> To be of two minds, undecided, or have two masters.
>
> (Psalm 119:113; Matthew 6:24; James 1:6-8, 22)

Double/Two-edge Sword

> A sword with 2 cutting blades, or edges, for use as both a shield and weapon; 2. The possibility of either a favorable or an unfavorable outcome.
>
> (Judges 3:16; Psalm 149:6; Proverbs 5:3-4; Hebrews 4:12; Revelation 1:16, 2:12)

Doubt

> Hope dimmed by fear, discouragement, or delay; 2. Conflicting beliefs or expectations; 3. The suspension of belief.
>
> (Genesis 17:15-17, 18:10-12; Exodus 5:22-23; Judges 6:15; Job 4:1-6; Psalm 31:22, 42:5-6, 43:5; Lamentations 3:17-18, 5:20-22; Matthew 28:17; Mark 4:40, 9:17-19, 16:11; Luke 8:25, 9:38-41, 23:10-11; John 20:24-25; James 1:5-8)

Dragon (Great)

> The ancient serpent known as Hasatan (Satan), the devil, the Great (scarlet) Beast with seven heads and ten horns, the angel of the bottomless pit, Abaddon, and Apollyon; 2. The accuser of those who keep the commandments of GOD and hold to the testimony of Jesus; 3. The Day Star, son of Dawn; 4. The little horn.
>
> (Revelation 8:10, 9:11, 12:1-17; 16:13, 20:1-3, 7-10; Genesis 3:1-15; Job 1:6-12, 2:1-6; Isaiah 14:12-14; Daniel 7:8, 8:9-11a; Zechariah 3:1; Matthew 25:41; Luke 10:18; John 8:44; Ephesians 2:1-2, 6:10-13; Jude 1:6)
>
> - A great scarlet dragon with seven heads and ten horns, a crown on each of the seven heads, stands before a woman about to give birth, ready to kill the child the moment it's born. This is in keeping with GOD's intent to put opposition and hostility between the woman and the serpent (Genesis 3:15). In rage or spite, the dragon sweeps

down a third of the stars of heaven onto the Earth. The Woman gives birth to a male child, who is immediately caught up to the throne of GOD. The Woman is given wings so that she may safely fly off into the surrounding wilderness to a place GOD has prepared for her, where she is nourished for 1,260 days. Furious, the dragon makes war with the rest of her offspring (Revelation 12:1-6, 13-17).

- A war begins in heaven. Michael the archangel and his angels are fighting the dragon and its angels. If stars represent angels, as Revelation 1:20 affirms, the dragon has wiped out one-third of Michael's army before war even begins. The dragon is nevertheless defeated, and he and his angels are cast down to the Earth (Revelation 12:7-9).
- Knowing it has very little time left, the dragon is determined to hunt down the rest of the Woman's offspring, those who keep the commandments of GOD and hold to the testimony of Jesus. For a time, it stands on the sandy floor at the bottom of the sea, before creating a beast in its own image. (Revelation 12:13-13:1).

Drunk with the Wine of the World

To be consumed by an intoxicating spirit of ambition, misspending, and self-indulgence.

(Genesis 11:1-4; Luke 21:34; Revelation 17:1-2, 18:2-3)

Earth Dwellers

Those who dwell on the earth.

(Revelation 3:10, 11:10, 14:6 [compare with 1 Kings 8:27, Revelation 13:6 and 21:3)

Edom

The country where Esau (brother of Jacob) lived in the land of Seir; 2. Biblical empire of the Edomites, descendants of Esau; 3. Esau marries a daughter of Ishmael, his half-uncle and the eldest son of Abraham, Esau's grandfather.

(Genesis 28:6-9, 32:3, 36:8-43; Numbers 20:14-21;1 Samuel 14:47; 2 Samuel 8:13-14; 1 Kings 11:14; 1 Chronicles 18:12-13; Jeremiah

49:7-11; Lamentations 4:21-22; Ezekiel 25:12-14; Daniel 11:41, Obadiah 1-21; Malachi 1:2-5)

Elect/Election

>A term expressing the idea or belief that GOD's love for all people also favors some particular individuals and groups over others; 2. Called by GOD to salvation; 3. One chosen for special favor as a vehicle for divine purposes; 4. The chosen; 5. The first fruits of GOD and the Lamb.

>(Genesis 18:17-19; Exodus 19:3-6a; Psalm 139:13-18; Isaiah 45:4, 42:1, 65:8-9; Matthew 1:18-23, 22:11-14, 24:22; Mark 13:20; Luke 10:22, 14:12-24, 18:6-8, 23:35; John 3:16, 6:45, 65, 8:28-30, 10:25-29, 15:16, 17:9; Acts 13:48; Romans 8:28-30, 9:11, 10:13, 11:7-10 [9:1-11:10]; Ephesians 1:1-14; Colossians 1:21-23; 2 Thessalonians 2:13-14, 2 Timothy 1:8-12; Titus 1:1-2; 2 John 1:1-2; Revelation 17:14, 20:4)

Empire (Kingdom)

>An established domain or territory held in check by, or under the authority of, one or more elected, appointed or self-appointed rulers or leaders.

>(Genesis 11:4-5; Ezekiel 38:1-3; Ezra 5:12; Daniel 1:1-2, 2:44, 7:24, 8:1, 20-25, 9:1, 10:1; Revelation 13:1, 18:2-3, 9,19)

Encouraged

>Internal courage and confidence.

>(Deuteronomy 31:7-8; Joshua 1:9; 1Samuel 30:6; Psalm 23:4, 31:24, 34:4, 121; Isaiah 41:10; John 16:32-33; Luke 12:4-7; Romans 8:31, 15:4; 1 Corinthians 15:50-58; 2 Corinthians 4:16-18)

End Times

>A progressive and steadily increasing time of trouble, chaos and tribulation leading to the Day of the Lord's Second Coming and the pouring out of GOD's vengeance on the earth.

>(Deuteronomy 32:35; Isaiah 46:10; Daniel 9:26-27, 12:1-4; Joel 2:28-32; Matthew 24:3-13,21-22, 36; Luke 21:25-28; Acts 17:30-

31; Romans 12:19; 2 Thessalonians 2:3-12; 2 Timothy 3:1-5; 2 Peter 3:3-7; 1 John 2:18; Revelation 6:1-17, 15:1, 18:1-24)

Endurance

The measuring and testing of faith over a period of time so as to be proven genuine or not; 2. The stamina necessary to compete or reach the end.

(Psalm 139:23-24; Isaiah 40:30-31; Daniel 1:8-16; Matthew 24:13; Luke 18:6-8, 23:44-46; Romans 5:1-5, 15:4; 1 Corinthians 13:4-7; 2 Timothy 4:7; Hebrews 6:11-12, 12:1-3; James 1:2-4, 12, 5:11; 1 Peter 2:19-20, 5:6-11; Revelation 1:9, 2:2-3,19, 3:10-11, 13:10, 14:12)

Envy

The desire to be the imagined greatness of someone else or to have what they have.

(Genesis 26:14; Exodus 20:17; Psalm 37:1-2, 7; Proverbs 14:30, 23:17, 24:1-2; Ecclesiastes 4:4; Mark 15:10; John 12:43; Acts 13:44-45, 17:4-9; James 3:16, 4:1-3; 3 John 1:9-10)

Esau and Jacob

Twin sons of Isaac and Rebekah. Jacob is the son favored by Rebekah, but Isaac favors Esau. Tension between the brothers begins in the womb and increases as they grow older, including an act of deception. Esau, recklessly (or in jest), agrees to give Jacob his inheritance rights as the eldest and firstborn son in exchange for a bowl of stew. When he is given the stew and loses his firstborn rights, Esau vows to kill Jacob. When the two brothers meet again after many years of estrangement they are able to reconcile, but Jacob is still afraid of his brother despite their reunion. He chooses not to follow Esau into the land of Canaan and settles far away instead, giving as his reason that their possessions together are too great for the land to support. Both become fathers of great nations.

(Genesis 25:20-34, 26:34-33:20, 35:1, 36:1-8)

Eternal Life

> The final destination for the saints, slaves and servants of GOD and Jesus the Christ, and the multitude who come from every nation, all tribes, peoples and languages; 2. To be in the-presence-of-God-without-end; 3. Everlasting life; 4. The reward for all who faithfully endure to the end.
>
> (Daniel 12:2; Matthew 25:34, 41; John 5:25-29; Romans 6:23; 1 John 5:11, 13; Revelation 7:9, 21:3-4)

Evil

> A life-threatening and life-taking belief system; 2. The hater of light; 3. The adversary of love; 4. The enemy of all things good.
>
> (Genesis 6:5-8; 50:15-20; 1 Samuel 12:19-22; 1 Kings 14:7-9; Psalm 5:4-6, 52; Proverbs 6:16-19, 8:13, 16:4, 21:15; Isaiah 5:20-21, 32:6-7; Zechariah 7:9-10; Matthew 12:33-37; Mark 7:20-23; John 3:20, 17:15; Romans 12:9; 1 Thessalonians 5:15, 21-22; 1 Timothy 6:10; 2 Timothy 3:1-5; James 1:13-15, 4:7-10; 1 John 5:18-19; Revelation 11:15)

Ezer

> A being capable of actively intervening on behalf of someone else, coming alongside them to support and help in their hour of need.
>
> (Genesis 2:18, 20; Exodus 18:4; Deuteronomy 33:7, 26, 29; Psalm 20:2, 33:20, 70:5, 89:19; 119:9-11, 121:1-2, 124:8, 146:5; Ezekiel 12:14; Daniel 11:34; Hosea 13:9)

False Prophet (see Second Beast)

False Teacher

> A morally corrupted mind from which truth has been taken away; 2. Someone who uses godly behavior as a way to game the system, gain possession of something, or capitalize on someone else.
>
> (Deuteronomy 18:20-22; Psalm 50:19-20; Jeremiah 14:14, 23:14-17; Ezekiel 13:9, 22:28; Lamentations 2:14; Daniel 7:25; Matthew 7:15, 23:27-28, 24; Mark 13:22-23; Luke 6:26; Acts 13:6, 20:29; Romans 16:17-18; 2 Corinthians 11:12-15; 1 Timothy 4:1-5; 2

Timothy 4:3-4; 2 Peter 2:1-3; Revelation 2:2, 13:11-17, 16:13-14, 19:20, 20:7-10)

Faith

The courage to say yes without knowing all the details for certain; 2. Persistent hope until one believes or knows for certain; 3. The endurance needed to bother going on and holding on no matter how long it takes; 4. The process of assessing options, choosing as wisely as one can and moving forward despite one's current doubts and uncertainties; 5. Experiencing difficulty while simultaneously hoping there is something good still to come; 6. Grace to believe you will receive every blessing that is for you.

(Genesis 12:1, 4; 1 Kings 17:8-16; Psalm 119:30; Proverbs 3:5-6; Isaiah 40:29-31; Matthew 9:27-30a; 15:21-28; Mark 11:22-24; 2 Corinthians 7; Ephesians 2:8-9; Philippians 4:12-13; Hebrews 11:1, 6; James 2:14-17; 1 John 5:4)

Favor

A special emphasis on, or affection for, another.

(Genesis 6:5-8, 39:20-22; Ezra 7:6, 27-28; Exodus 12:35-36, 33:12-13; Psalm 5:12, 30:5-7, 84:11, 106:4-5; Proverbs 3:1-4, 13:15; Isaiah 60:10; Jeremiah 29:11; Luke 2:40, 52, 14:12-14; John 3:16; Acts 2:46-47; Romans 8:28-30; Hebrews 4:16)

Fear

Fainting of the soul from within; 2. The by-product of one's imagination being held hostage by the most terrible, imagined possibilities; 3. The emotion most often responsible for persuading one to hold back what should be given without being asked; 4. A power strong enough to compel one to yield.

(Exodus 12:29-32, 14:10-14; Deuteronomy 31:6; Joshua 1:9; Psalm 34:4; Proverbs 29:25; Mark 5:36; 6:48-50; Luke 12:22-23, 22:43-44; John 20:19; 2 Timothy 1:7; 1 Peter 3:14-17; Revelation 2:10-11)

Fear of the Lord

>The healthy and appropriate response to the power of GOD; 2. Wisdom's first lesson; 3. The recognition and understanding that one's intimacy with GOD is surpassed only by the Majesty of GOD.
>
>(Deuteronomy 10:12-13; Psalm 103:13; Proverbs 8:13, 9:10, 14:26, 19:23; Ecclesiastes 12:13-14; Matthew 10:28; Luke 1:50)

First Fruits

>The best or most outstanding cream of the crop from the fruits of one's labor (i.e. faithful obedience, produce from the ground or trees, livestock commodities, income, etc.).
>
>(Exodus 22:29-30; Leviticus 23:9-12; Numbers 18:12; 2 King 4:42; 2 Chronicles 31:5a; Psalm 105:36; Proverbs 3:9; Jeremiah 2:3; Ezekiel 44:30-31; Romans 11:16; 1 Corinthians 15:20-23; 2 Thessalonians 2:13; James 1:18; Revelation 14:4-5)

Flesh and Spirit

>The war going on between one's mortal body and divine spirit; 2. The internal tension felt when having to choose between doing a pleasurable thing or fulfilling the demand of righteousness.
>
>(Mark 14:38; John 3:5-7, 6:35, 60-63; Romans 7:18-25; 1 Corinthians 6:13-20, 15:50; Galatians 5:17; 1 John 2:15-16, 3:9)

Food and Water

>Literal and metaphorical elements essential for the sustenance of physical and spiritual life.
>
>(Genesis 1:29, 9:3; Deuteronomy 8:3; Ecclesiastes 3:12-13; Matthew 4:1-4; John 4:1-11, 6:35; 1 Timothy 6:8)

Forgiveness

>Dropping the stone one has been holding in their hand; 2. Uncurling one's fingers from around an adversary's throat.
>
>(Genesis 50:15-21; 1 Kings 8:46-51; 2 Chronicles 30:9; Nehemiah 9:30-31; Jonah 3:10; Proverbs 10:12, 25:21; Matthew 6:12, 18:23-27; Mark 11:25; Luke 17:3-4; John 8:1-9; Acts 7:54-60; Romans

13:17; 2 Corinthians 2:5-8; Ephesians 5:31-32; Colossians 3:12-13; Hebrews 10:15-17)

Four Living Creatures

> Four guardian angels positioned around the four sides of the heavenly throne. They have eyes in the front, behind and all around, and have the appearance of a lion, an ox, a man, and an eagle in flight. Each creature has six wings and constantly praises GOD. Some similarities exist between these four guardian angels and the four beasts mention in Daniel 7:3-7, but in an unholy and monstrous way.
>
> (Revelation 4:5-8, 5:6-14, 6:1, 14:1-3, 15:7, 19:4; Isaiah 6:1-3)

Freedom in Christ

> Deliverance from the law of sin and death and the yoke of slavery; 2. The gift of free rein and self-determination to believe what one will; 3. The right to walk according to the Spirit of life.
>
> (Isaiah 61:1; Psalm 118:5, 119:45; Luke 4:18-19; John 8:31-38; Acts 13:38-39; Romans 8:1-4; 1 Corinthians 6:12, 9:19, 10:23-33; Galatians 2:4, 4:1-7, 5:1, 13, Hebrews 2:14-15; 1 Peter 2:16)

Fruit

> The reproductive part of a plant or seed that has ripened and is now ready to eat, especially the kind grown on branches above ground (apples, oranges, pears, figs, etc.; 2. The visible effects and results of a person's efforts, presence and purpose in the world.
>
> (Genesis 1:28b, 3:6; Jeremiah 17:7-8; Matthew 3:8, 7:15-16a, 12:33; Luke 13:6-9; John 15:1-2, 8; Galatians 5:22-23; Colossians 1:10)

Gentile

> A non-Jew; 2. An identifier signifying that a person is not Jewish; 3. The non-Jewish nation out of which GOD will form a people through faith.
>
> (Genesis 5:32, 7:1, 9:8-17, 10:1—Noah was the father of Shem, Ham and Japheth, from whom many nations on earth are descended—Isaiah 56:6-8; Matthew 10:5-6; John 10:14-15; Acts 15:12-17; Romans 3:8-9, 28-30; Galatians 3:7-9)

GOD

> I AM WHO I AM; 2. A descriptive title reserved for the unseen Creator of all things who will not be held hostage to, or by, the religious beliefs of any nation, tribe, religious person, or sect. This is in contrast to the God-in-the-Bible as understood by humans; 3. The energy force which existed before the human design became a thought; 4. The One who keeps and loves those who love and obey GOD; 5. The LORD.
>
> (Genesis 1:1-2, 26a, 27, 31, 2:4; Exodus 3:13-15; Daniel 1:8-9, 9:4; Acts 17:22-28)

Godly

> One whose ultimate concerns are the will and ways of GOD.
>
> (Psalm 1:1-2; Zephaniah 3: 12-13; Matthew 5: 2-12, 6:14-15; Ephesians 4:17-5:21; Philippians 4:6-7; 2 Peter 1:3-11, 16-19; Revelation 14:4-5)

Godlessness (in the last days)

> The end time when false teachers and the unrepentant who are corrupted in mind and behavior will emerge throughout the world in full force.
>
> (Matthew 24:1-24; 1 Timothy 4:1-3; 2 Timothy 3:1-5; 2 Peter 3:1-10; Revelation 11:2, 13:5-8, 11-17)

Godly Hope

> Confidence that GOD can and will do something.
>
> (Psalm 130:5-6; Isaiah 40:31; Luke 8:40-50, 18:35-42)

Going out and Coming in

> One's daily comings and goings; 2. A period of time.
>
> (1 Samuel 2:9; Deuteronomy 28:1, 6; Joshua 6:1; Psalm 18:31-36, 37:23-24, 84:11-12, 119:1-3, 121:7-8; Daniel 9:25a; Matthew 6:13; John 10:9)

Gospels

> Term meaning 'good news'; 2. The good news reports confirming that GOD's promise to send a Savior (Messiah) has been fulfilled; 3. The collection of New Testament books known as Matthew, Mark, Luke and John.
>
> (Genesis 12:1-3; Isaiah 7:14, 9:6; Jeremiah 23:5; Micah 5:2; Zechariah 9:9; Matthew 1: 18-23; Luke 1:26-33; John 1:35-45; Acts 13:16-23)

Grace (GOD's)

> Goodness shown by GOD toward the undeserving; 2. The dominant attribute of GOD when holiness is at odds with humanity; 3. GOD's frequent supercalifragilisticexpialidocious response to wrongdoing.
>
> (Genesis 6:8; Judges 10:10, 15-16; Zechariah 12:10; John 1:17; Romans 3:20-24, 5:8; Ephesians 2:8-9; 2 Timothy 1:8-10)

Gratitude

> Overflowing appreciation and thanksgiving.
>
> (2 Samuel 6:12-14a; Luke 17:11-16)

Great City (The)

> Jerusalem and/or the contemporary Babylon (i.e. America).
>
> (Matthew 23:34-39; Luke 13:31-35; Revelation 11:7-8, 16:19, 17:18, 18)

Great Prince of the Hosts of Heaven

> Jesus the Christ.
>
> (Daniel 8:11)

Hasatan

> The Hebrew word for The Adversary or The Prosecutor. Also referred to as The Tempter, The Devil and The Dragon. The definite article 'the' indicates the word is a function, rather than a proper name.

(1 Chronicles 21:1-4; Job 1:1-12, 2:1-6; Zechariah 3:1-5; Matthew 4:1-11; John 8:39-47; 1 Peter 5:8-9; 1 John 3:8; Jude 1:9; Revelation 12:7-12)

Hate

A violent posture or attitude of the heart; 2. To reject completely; 3. The appropriate response toward what is false, evil, or wicked.

(Leviticus 19:17; Psalm 5:4-5, 97:10, 101:3, 139:21-22; Proverbs 6:16-19; Ecclesiastes 3:1, 8; Isaiah 66:5; Amos 5:21; Matthew 5:43-48, 6:24, 12:46-50; Luke 14:25-27; John 7:7, 12:25, 15:18-19, 25; Romans 12:9; James 4:4; 1 John 2:9-11, 15-17, 4:20-21; Revelation 2:6)

Heaven

A term used to describe the place where GOD resides; 2. All of one's happiest, imagined possibilities becoming real; 3. Where the future is born.

(Genesis 28:16-17; Isaiah 25:6-9, 65:17; Matthew 7:21-23; Luke 15:7; John 14:1-7; 2 Corinthians 5;1-5; Philippians 3:20-21; Colossians 1:13; 2 Peter 3:13; Revelation 7:9-12, 15-17, 20:1, 21:1-8)

Holiness

The mirror-image of GOD.

(Leviticus 19:1-2; Matthew 5:48)

Holy of Holies

The most holy inner place or sanctuary where GOD meets with individuals one-on-one in prayer and conversation.

(Exodus 26:33; Mark 15:38; Hebrews 9:3, 11-14)

Honesty

When thought, speech and conduct all agree with one another.

(Genesis 30:33; 2 Kings 12:13-15; Hebrews 13:18)

Hope

> The chance a possibility still exists.
>
> (1 Samuel 1:10, 17-18; Psalms 38:15; Isaiah 40:31; Jeremiah 29:11; Mark 9:23; Hebrews 10:23)

Hour has Come (The)

> The coming or approaching time of birth, death or deliverance.
>
> (Esther 4:14; Mark 14:41b; John 2:4, 7:6, 30, 8:20; 12:23, 16:21, 17:1, 19:30; 2 Timothy 4:6; Revelation 3:10, 14:15)

Hypocrite/Hypocrisy

> To play the part of, or pretend to be, someone deserving of trust; 2. To make an ugly face look sweet; 3. Speech that does not match practice.
>
> (Isaiah 29:13; Psalm 55:21; Matthew 23:1-3; Mark 7:6-7; Romans 2:3, 21-24)

I am the Way, the Truth and the Life

> Scriptural statement reportedly spoken by Jesus which many Christians use as proof-text that one must be a Christian to be saved from the second death and enter eternal life. This is inconsistent with the statement itself, which clarifies that Jesus alone gets to decide who's in and who's out. Signifying that every person standing before the throne for judgment has a chance if Jesus is on their side.

Immediately

> The fierce urgency of <u>now</u>.
>
> (Genesis 27:43-44; Mark 4:16)

In, but not of, the World

> Inhabiting the Earth as a particular person in the world, without assimilating or becoming part of the world's belief system.
>
> (John 17:6a, 14-16; Ephesians 6:12-20; 1 John 4:4-6)

Inclusion

> There is always room for one more at the table.
>
> (Luke 14:13-14; Acts 10:9-48; Romans 15:7; Galatians 3:28; Philippians 2:3-4; Hebrews 13:2; James 2:1-9)

Insider

> A hearer or listener with inside-information about the mysteries of GOD; 2. An emerging social term for a person living on the inside of prison.
>
> (Jeremiah 1:11-14; Matthew 13:10; Mark 4:10-16; Luke 8:9-15; John 16:12-15; Revelation 7:13-14)

Israel

> The name given to Jacob by a man who lost a wrestling match with him; 2. The descendants of Abraham, Isaac and Jacob; 3. Israel the land received by Abraham and passed down through Isaac; 3. The nation, or house, of Israel; 4. The children of Israel; 5. The outcasts of Israel; 6. The restoration of Israel; 7. GOD's people Israel, gathered from every nation, tribe, people and language; 8. GOD's glory.
>
> (Genesis 28:13-14, 32:28, 35:10; Exodus 15:22; Leviticus 25:1-2; Psalm 33:12; Isaiah 11:12, 46:12-13; Jeremiah 31:31; Ezekiel 11:17, 37:21; Amos 9:11-15; Matthew 3:9, 10:5-6, 15:24; Galatians 3:29; Romans 11:25-27; Revelation 7:9)

Jacob (see Esau and Jacob)

Jerusalem

> The city of the great King.
>
> (Matthew 5:33-34)

Jesus (Yeshua) of Nazareth

> The living WORD of GOD; 2. GOD's Son and promised Savior; 3. The ancient Jewish Rabbi, Prophet and Priest who was arrested and executed on a cross for crimes He did not commit; 4. Michael, the great Prince.

(Isaiah 53:7-12; Daniel 12:1-2; Matthew 26:57, 59-60, 27:1-2, 24-26; Mark 14:45a, 55-59, 15:6-15; Luke 22:70-71, 23:4, 13-16, 20-25, 26; John 3:17, 18:12, 38b-40, 19:4, 6, 12a, 16; Acts 13:13-23; 1 John 4:14, Titus 2:11)

Jew

A descendant from the tribe of Judah, one subset of the twelve tribes constituting the children of Israel (*Jew/Judah* and *Israel* are not interchangeable). Jesus of Nazareth, through His parents and king David, was a descendant of Judah.

(Isaiah 66:5-14; Jeremiah 31:31-32; John 4:7-29, 39-42; Luke 3:10-14, 10:30, 33-37; Acts 13:13-23; Romans 2:17-20, 16:17-20; Galatians 3:7, 23-29; Revelation 2:9, 3:9, 7:4-8)

Jews

Descendants of Abraham who do not believe or accept Jesus of Nazareth to be Israel's Savior.

(Isaiah 66:1-4; Jeremiah 31:31-34; Matthew 3:7-10, 12:33-37, 27:24-25; Luke 3:7-9, 10:25-32, 22:66-70; John 5:18, 8:31-47; Acts: 13:4-12, 17:1-15, 21:20; 1 Romans 2:17-28, 10:10-13, 11:1-10, 13-14; 1 Thessalonians 2:13-16 and 4:1-5)

Jezebel

An adversary and enemy of GOD; 2. The power behind the Earthly throne, as the Woman clothed with the sun, a moon under her feet, and twelve stars crowning her head is divine among the hosts of heaven.

(1 Kings 16:29-33, 18:13-19, 21:20-23; 2 Kings 9:30-37; Revelation 12:1-6, 13-17)

Joy

A spirit of rejoicing or victory.

(2 Samuel 6:14a; Isaiah 9:2-7; John 16:21-22; Revelation 19:1-5)

Judah

> The fourth son of Jacob and Leah, his first (and unloved) wife. Contrary to Genesis 37:9, Judah becomes the inheritor of the eldest son's portion, and is father of the descendants who give birth to GOD's promise Messiah.
>
> (Genesis 29:15-25, 31, 35, 37:1-11, 49:1, 8-12; Hebrews 7:11-14; 1 Thessalonians 2:14a, Revelation 5:5, 7:5)

Judgement (GOD's)

> The dispensation of Holy and Righteous Justice.
>
> (Psalm 7:11; John 5:21-27; Matthew 12:36-37; Revelation 20:11-15)

Judgement (Human)

> An elected, appointed or self-appointed judge who interprets and applies meaning, significance and value to the law or lives of others.
>
> (Genesis 11:1-4; 1 Chronicles 21:1-3; John 8:15-16; James 2:1-4)

Just

> What one is entitled to; 2. Taking what's needed without taking more than one's fair share.
>
> (Leviticus 19:35-36, 25:17; Deuteronomy 25:13-15; Proverbs 11:1; Acts 4:32, 34-35: Ephesians 4:28; Revelation 16:5-6)

Just and Unjust

> Righteous prey and wicked hunter, respectively.
>
> (Psalm 10:2-11; Proverbs 29:27; Ecclesiastes 3:16-17, 7:15, 9:1-2; Matthew 5:43-45)

Justice

> The opposite of injustice; 2. That which must be done to ensure that what's just is done.
>
> (Leviticus 19:15; Proverbs 21:15; Luke 18:7; Hebrews 10:30; Romans 12:19)

Justified

> To be proven that one's reasons are just, right and reasonable grounds; 2. To be declared righteous in the sight of GOD.
>
> (Genesis 15:6; 1 Samuel 15:3; Isaiah 2:1-4; Mark 16:16; John 10:9, 15:6; Romans 3:21-26, 5:1, 9:15-16; Galatians 5:6; Ephesians 2:8-10)

Keeper

> One who guards and protects; 2. Someone who responds to the needs of others.
>
> (Genesis 4:2; Psalm 121:8; Zechariah 7:9-10; Matthew 9:36; Luke 10:36-37; John 10:11, 16; 1 Corinthians 10:24; Galatians 6:2; Philippians 2:3-4; Revelations 7:15-17)

Key(s)

> A symbol of authority; 2. The key to the kingdom of GOD; 3. The handing over of keys (i.e. Matthew 16:19) signifies a dispensation of the new order of things. At His death and resurrection, Jesus gains authority over the powers of death and the underworld, and gains control of the keys to the prison restraining death and Hades. When the abyss is opened, the powers below come out and are used as instruments of GOD's judgement, assembled for battle on the great day of GOD the Almighty, after which the enemy receives judgement. This is similar to how GOD used Israel's enemies to instigate war with Israel, a means to test whether the nation would obey the commandments of the LORD. After the war was over, the enemy was often destroyed for the harm it had caused Israel.
>
> (Judges 3:24-25, 10:1-16, 29-32; Isaiah 22:20-22, 43:19; Zechariah 9:1-17; Matthew 16:13-29; Luke 11:52; Acts 14:27; Revelation 1:18, 3:7, 9:1-3 (the first Woe), 11, 16:13-14, 20:1-3)

Knowledge

> Learning that accompanies and complements faith.
>
> (Hosea 6:6; Proverbs 2:6, 8:10-11; John 8:32; Acts 17:11)

Lack of Love

> Gratifying one's own needs and desires at the expense of someone else.
>
> (Genesis 4:8; Matthew 24:12; 1 Corinthians 13:1-3;1 John 3:16-18, 4:19-21; Revelation 2:4)

Lamb

> A baby sheep; 2. A symbol of innocence; 3. A holy symbol of Jesus the Messiah.
>
> (Isaiah 53:7; John 1:29,36; 1 Peter 1:18-19; Revelation 5:1-14, 7:10, 13:8, 19:9, 21:9, 27)

Lamb's Book of Life (The Book of Life of the Lamb That Was Slain)

> On the day the dead stand before the throne of GOD, a series of books are opened and the dead are judged according to what is written in the books. Anyone whose name not found written in the Lamb's Book of Life is thrown into the lake of fire.
>
> (Exodus 32:31-32; Daniel 12:1-3; Revelation 13:7-8, 20:11-15)

Lamp (see Light)

Law (The Perfect) (also see Command)

> The law of liberty; 2. The law of the Lord; 3. The freedom one receives as a result of faith in Yeshua/Jesus of Nazareth.
>
> (Psalm 118:5, 119:45; Isaiah 61:1-2; Matthew 11:28-30; Luke 4:18-19; John 8:34-36, 10:10,14:6; Acts 13:38-39, 15:1, 5-11; Romans 6:15-18, 20-23, 7:4-6, 8:1-4; 1 Corinthians 6:12, 8:9; Galatians 2:20-21, 4:23-26, 5:1, 13-15; Hebrews 9:15; James 1:25, 2:10-12)

Lawless Ones

> Those who make a practice of sinning.
>
> (1 John 3:4)

Lean Not On Your Own Understanding

> Listening to the voices of reason and caution, mindful of their limitations, and staying open to the possibility of being wrong; 2. The willingness to say "Lord/Sir/Ma'am, you know", and watch for what's not known to be revealed, when GOD makes things plain and clear.
>
> (Isaiah 37:1-3; Numbers 22:21-33; Proverbs 3:5; 2 Timothy 2:1-7; Revelation 7:13-14)

Life (Mortal)

> All that happens between birth and death; 2. How things just are.
>
> (Ecclesiastes 3:1-8; Matthew 6:25-34)

Light/Lamp

> A lit or lighted lamp that illuminates, reveals and enables others to see; 2. That which separates day from night; 3. Light is responsible for all of life on Earth, without which all living things would cease to exist; 4. The offspring of Love and Duty.
>
> (Genesis 1:3-5, 14-19; Psalm 119:105; Matthew 5:13-16; Luke 11:33; John 1:1-9, 3:19-21, 8:12, 9:1-5; Philippians 2:14-15; 2 Timothy 1:8-12)

Living (or Walking) Dead

> One who is physically alive but spiritually asleep, or dead.
>
> (Ecclesiastes 9:5-6; Isaiah 6:8-10; Matthew 8:22; Luke 15:24; 1 Timothy 5:5-6; Revelation 3:1-2)

Lo (see Behold)

Longing

> Envisioning or desiring beyond a given reality.
>
> (Genesis 31:30; 2 Samuel 23:15; Psalms 107:9, Proverbs 13:12; Matthew 5:2-11; Luke 12:13-21)

Lord (*Kurios*)

> The GOD or god one has chosen to follow and obey; 2. A title designating *Master*, modified to *Mister* circa 16th century and subsequently abbreviated to *Mr*.
>
> (Deuteronomy 6:4-5; Amos 5:14-15; Mark 2:25-28; Philippians 2:5-11)

Lord of the Earth

> Signifies divine authority, sovereignty and dominion over the world and its creations.
>
> (Genesis 1:26; Psalm 24:1; Zechariah 4:14; Matthew 24:4-5; Revelation 11:4)

Love

> The fulfilling of the Law; 2. The crown of brotherly affection; 3. Intimacy, passion and deep affection for another; 4. Compassion capable of separating "What you did is unacceptable" from "But everything will be ok".
>
> (Leviticus 19:17-18; Psalm 91:1-16; Isaiah 49:14-16; John 13:34-35; Romans 8:38-39, 13:8-12; 2 Peter 1:7; 1 John 4:7-11, 16-19; Revelation 2:4-5)

Lust

> An intense and unquenchable desire to achieve, acquire, borrow and take even more.
>
> (Genesis 3:6; Numbers 15:39; Luke 12:13-15; 1 John 2:15-17)

Man

> The male half of humankind created in GOD's image; 2. The *y* (male) chromosome lineage has been studied and traced to "Y Chromosome Adam," reported to be more than 70,000 years younger than "Mitochondrial Eve."
>
> (Genesis 1:27, 2:5-8, 15, 20-23, 5:1-6:14)

- In the first creation story, both the woman and man are created simultaneously, stand together before GOD, and receive the same charges and list of responsibilities (Genesis 1:26-30).

- In the second creation story, GOD first creates a man, decides it's not good for the man to be alone, and creates a woman out of the man's body (Genesis 2:5-23).

- In the third creation story, on the day GOD creates humankind in the image of the Creator, GOD takes on male form and becomes "he". Additionally, the lack of a definite article before the term <u>Adam</u> suggests it's meant as a proper noun—a name—rather than a title (Genesis 5:1-2). From then on, the voice and presence of the Woman is diminished or silenced in the Bible.

- When men began multiplying on the earth, they begin taking multiple women as wives. When GOD sees how great the wickedness of Man on the earth is, the decision is made to destroy all men because the earth is filled with such violence through them. Only a man named Noah finds favor in the eyes of GOD. Interestingly, when Jesus accuses the Jews of being children of the devil, they protest to Him that they were not born of sexual immorality (Genesis 6:1-8; John 8:39-47).

Mankind (Humankind)

    Created to oversee and care for the earth and the things in it, and to enjoy it all.

    (Genesis 1:26-29, 2:15; Ecclesiastes 7:14, 12:1-14)

Mark (see Seal)

Mature (in the Spirit)

    One having sharp powers of discernment, trained by practicing to distinguish good from evil; 2. Having teeth, able to eat solid food and digest hard things.

    (John 16:12-15; Hebrews 5:11-14)

Money

    Evil's nesting material.

    (Ecclesiastes 5:10; 1 Timothy 6:10; Revelation 3:17)

Morals

    Pursuing truth and justice above self-serving advancement.

    (Proverbs 11:3; Titus 2:7-8)

Mystery (of GOD)

    GOD has plans the world knows nothing about.

    (Job 11:7; 1 Corinthians 2:16; 1 Timothy 3:16; Revelation 4:1-2, 5:1-4)

Name

    The mark of personhood; 2. One's identification.

    (Exodus 3:13-14; Deuteronomy 5:11; Proverbs 22:1; Matthew 18:20; Mark 5:9; Revelation 2:17)

Nicolaitans

    A term representing a cult or religious practice that weakens the sanctity and faith of believers, diminishes the Church's witness, or fails to honor and respect the line separating the worship of GOD from the worship of idols. The biblical implication suggests the Nicolaitans were following in the footsteps of Balaam; 2. Followers who perverted the teachings of Nicolaus, a convert of Antioch who was selected as one of the first seven deacons.

    (Acts 6:5-6; Revelation 2:6, 15)

Nothing New Under the Sun

    Established alphabets and musical notes are rearranged to make 'new' words and songs, old materials are extracted from the earth, repurposed and reshaped to make 'new' items, and human emotions rotate from person to person like clockwork according to personal circumstances and world news events.

(Ecclesiastes 1:9-10)

New Things

According to GOD, the status quo no longer exist, no matter what things look like on the earth.

(Isaiah 42:9, 62:2, 65:17; Jeremiah 31:31-34; Ezekiel 36:25-27; Matthew 9:16-17, 13:51-52; John 13:34-35; Hebrews 10:19-22; Revelation 14:3, 21:5)

Obedience to God

Faithfully fulfilling GOD's itinerary and commands as one goes about the course of daily living in the world.

(Exodus 19:5-6; Deuteronomy 28:1-3; Luke 6:46-49, 11:27-28; John 21:3-6; Romans 6:16-19; 1 Corinthians 3:5; Revelation 1:3, 14:12)

Oneness

The mutual sharing of a common interest, love or goal.

(John 17:6-23; Ephesians 4:4-6; Philippians 2:2)

1,000 (One Thousand Year) Reign of Jesus

The one-thousand-year reign of Jesus as King. Reigning with Him are those who have the authority to judge the twelve tribes of Israel, those killed for delivering the testimony of Jesus and the WORD of GOD, and those who did not worship the beast or receive its mark on their foreheads or hands. During this same period of time, Hasatan is locked up in an otherworld prison. When the thousand years are ended, the devil is released and set loose to deceive the nations one final time and gather the nations together for battle against the saints of GOD, but to no avail. The nations warring against the saints are consumed by fire from heaven, and Hasatan is thrown into the lake of fire where the beast and false prophet are.

(Revelation 12:9, 17a; 20:4, 7-10)

1,260 Days (One Thousand, Two Hundred, Sixty Days)

Forty-two (42) months; 2. A time, times, and half a time.

(Daniel 7:25, 12:7-12; Revelation 11:1-3, 12:6, 14, 13:5)

1,290 Days (One Thousand, Two hundred, Ninety Days)

> Forty-three (43) months. For the sake of the elect the end days are cut short, from 1290 to 1260.
>
> (Daniel 12:11-12; Revelation 13:5)

1,335 Days (One Thousand, Three Hundred, Thirty-five Days)

> Forty-four and one-half (44 ½) months.
>
> (Daniel 12:11-12)

144,000 (One Hundred and Forty-four Thousand)

> The slaves of GOD; 2. The total number to be sealed and redeemed from humankind as first fruits for GOD and the Lamb, twelve thousand (12,000) from every tribe pertaining to the sons of Israel.
>
> (Revelation 7:1-8; 14:1-5)
>
> - Between the opening of the fifth and sixth seals, John sees four angels holding back the northern, southern, eastern and western winds, so that no wind might blow across the earth or across the sea. The absence of wind projects an illusion of calm or peace, but the wind being stilled (the absence of wind) also results in extreme temperature variations, erratic and unpredictable rainfall, droughts and flooding, buildup of pollution in certain areas, the decline or disappearance of pollination, and the disruption of the natural water cycle from rainfall. John sees another angel holding the seal of the living GOD, who directs the four angels to continue holding back the wind until the slaves (Gk. *doulous*) of GOD have been sealed on their foreheads (Revelation 7:1-4).

One with GOD

> To hold hands while walking in the garden with GOD; 2. "To respond to GOD as a violin responds to the bow of the master"—Frank C. Laubach
>
> (1 Kings 18:21; John 10:30, 17:20-21)

Opinion

>Words that contradict another person's lived experiences.

>(Proverbs 18:2; Romans 14:1-12)

Oppression

>The pressing down of suffering.

>(Judges 4:1-3; Proverbs 22:16; Isaiah 10:1-2; Jeremiah 22:13; Acts 7:34a; 2 Corinthians 6:3-10; James 2:6; Revelation 6:10)

Order (of End Time Events)

>A sequencing of biblical end time events according to the Book of Daniel and Book of Revelation. Daniel, a slave of GOD, belongs to the tribe of Judah. When Jerusalem was assaulted by king Nebuchadnezzar of Babylon, Daniel was taken prisoner, but he rose to become the third most important ruler in Babylon as a direct result of his faithfulness and obedience to GOD. John was a slave of Jesus the Christ. He received his vision while imprisoned on the island of Patmos for preaching the WORD of GOD and testimony of Jesus. Both Daniel and John receive visions of things which have already happened, things currently happening, and the order of things still to come.

>Daniel reports the Most High GOD has decreed seventy weeks to deal with Daniel's people and the holy city, finish the transgression, put an end to sin, atone for iniquity, usher in everlasting righteousness, seal both the vision and the prophet and anoint a (new) holy place. The revelation to John is from Jesus the Christ, who is speaking on behalf of GOD, who is passing information along to the slaves of GOD on Earth concerning things to come. The visions John receives and reveals to the church are filled with regular reminders to the faithful that only the one who endures and finishes the race wins a crown, and multiple warnings to those who are perishing.

>Thousands of years separate the lives and visions of Daniel and John, but almost identical language is used when each describes seeing a s/Son of man dressed in linen with a golden sash around His chest, having eyes like fire, legs and feet like burnished bronze and a roaring voice, and the sight causes both men to faint. When Daniel mentions a flood, it's reminiscent of the blood spoken of by John that flowed

from a winepress high as a horse's bridle. The image of a rainbow wrapped around GOD's throne, which John describes in his writing, conveys the sense of GOD willing GOD's Self to remember and keep the covenantal promise to never again use a flood to completely destroy the Earth and the people in it (Genesis 9:11-13).

In John's vision, he sees the New Jerusalem and mentions in detail twelve gates, twelve foundation walls, the jewels encrusted into the walls, and the river of the water of life flowing down the middle of the street. According to Daniel, before the sanctuary is restored to its rightful place, 2,300 evenings and mornings of tribulation must first pass (8:13-14). 1,290 of those days have been allotted to the time frame between when the regular burnt offering is taken away (circa 70 CE) and the abomination that makes desolate is set up, and blessed is the one who endures until day 1,335 (Daniel 12:11-12). In 1995, Congress adopted the Jerusalem Embassy Act to further an ongoing attempt to move the US Embassy to the city of Jerusalem. On May 14, 2018 (the 70th anniversary of the creation of the modern state of Israel), the US embassy was officially relocated from Tel Aviv and set up in Jerusalem. Interestingly, when 70 CE is subtracted from 2018 CE, the sum remaining is 1948, the year the modern state of Israel was created. When Jesus warned about the signs of the close of the age (end days), He said that when the abomination of desolation spoken of by Daniel was situated in the holy place (Jerusalem), the great tribulation would take place after that. For the sake of the elect, the number of those days is shortened (Matthew 24:15, 21-22). According to John, the first beast is allowed to exercise authority for 1,260 days, or 42 months (Revelation 13:5).

(Daniel 1:1-12:13; Revelation 1:1-22:21)

(Note: What should not be forgotten or made irrelevant is GOD's unchanging promise to bring the people of Judah and Israel back to the land given to their fathers, and have them take possession of it. That promise was fulfilled when the state of Israel was re-established in 1948, despite the people having broken their Covenant with GOD. GOD also promised to send a Savior into the world to rescue Israel from its iniquities, which was fulfilled when Yeshua/Jesus of Nazareth was born. When GOD's Savior is crucified and His blood is shed, the reckoning required for the life of man is fulfilled (Genesis 4:8, 9:5-6). These examples witness to GOD's capacity and ability to be faithful even when others are not. Having fulfilled the promises, GOD is now free to bring this generation to an end.

(Genesis 1:26, 3:22-24, 6:1-8, 9:1-17; Numbers 23:19; Deuteronomy 7:9, 30:1-20; Joshua 1:1-9, 7:1, 13:1, 23:1-16, 24:14-24; Jeremiah 30:1-3; Ezekiel 11:14-20, 16:59-63, 17:19-21, 36:16-24; Matthew 24:32-35; Mark 15:25, 16:9, 19-20; 2 Timothy 2:13; Hebrew 10:23)

The order of end time events according to the Book of Daniel aligned with the Book of Revelation:

- The prophet Daniel sees four great beasts and is particularly disturbed about the fourth beast, which is exceedingly strong, has ten horns and is different from the other three, but he doesn't share his concerns with anyone, not even Hananiah and Mishael (Daniel 1:1-7, 7:1-28; Revelation 13: 1-2a)
- Daniel has a disturbing second vision involving a ram, a goat and a little horn that becomes exceedingly great, even supreme towards the host of heaven. The little horn is so powerful it's able to throw some of the host and stars of heaven to the ground and trample on them. Daniel also sees an anointed one being destroyed by the great little horn, the end of regular burnt offering, the desecration of the sanctuary, and un-truth prospering. From the time the vision concerning the regular burnt offerings is given to Daniel, to the time the transgression is made desolate and the sanctuary is giving over and hosts are trampled underfoot is 2,300 evenings and morning (days and nights). When Daniel seeks understanding regarding the vision, the angel Gabriel arrives to tell him what it all means and that the vision is for the time of the end, many days in the future, but even with the explanation Daniel still doesn't understand (Daniel 8:1-27; Revelation 7:13, 11:1-2, 12:3-4a)
- Daniel diligently seeks GOD in fasting and confessional prayer, wearing sackcloth and ashes and praying fervently that he might understand the vision. His prayers are heard and Gabriel returns bringing an answer (Daniel 9:1-23 [see Jeremiah 33:3])

- Gabriel informs Daniel about the decree of <u>seventy weeks.</u> From the going out of the word to restore and rebuild Jerusalem to the coming of an anointed prince shall be <u>seven weeks</u>. For <u>sixty-two weeks</u> Jerusalem will reestablished and reformed, but it will be done during times of trouble. During the remaining <u>one week,</u> an anointed one is finished off, the destroyer appears, desolations are decreed, the one who makes life desolate is destroyed at the decreed end time, and to the end there will be war (Daniel 9:24-27)
- In the third year of king Cyrus of Persia's reign, Daniel receives word the king has decreed that Jerusalem and the temple are to be rebuilt, at which point he understands the visions and what Gabriel had been trying to tell him are true, and he becomes ill from the knowledge. Daniel sees another vision, this time involving a man dressed in linen with belt of gold around His waist with fire in His eyes, arms and legs of burnished bronze, and having a loud voice. One with the appearance of a child of man touches Daniel's lips when he becomes unresponsive from shock. The man clothed in linen explains to Daniel the events that are to take place during his own time and assures him about the future of his people. Those names found in the book will be delivered. Daniel is told not to worry about the outcome but to go on living his life, because the WORDS have been sealed until the time of the end. From the time the regular burnt offering is taken away (circa 70 CE, when the second temple is destroyed) and the abomination that makes desolate is set up there shall be 1,290 days, and war will be present until the end (Daniel 10:1-12:13; <u>Revelation 5:1-4, 13:7-12, 20:7-15</u>)

The order of end time events according to the Book of Revelation aligned with Daniel's vision:

- John is instructed to write seven letters to seven churches which are dictated by Jesus the Christ. Each recipient of a letter is advised to hear what's being said to the other six churches (Revelation 1:1-3:22; <u>Daniel 9:1-19</u>)

- John hears a trumpet-like voice behind him. When he turns to see who's speaking, he sees one like a Son of Man clothed in a long white robe with hair the color of snow, a golden sash around His chest and feet like burnished bronze refined in a furnace, and John faints are the sight of Him (Revelation 4:1-11; Daniel 10:5-7)
- There is a degree of despair in heaven because no one has been found worthy to open the sealed scroll containing the WORDS (the mystery) of GOD—and then good news is heard! The Lion of the tribe of Judah, the Root of David, has conquered and become worthy to open the seals! The Lion approaches the heavenly throne dressed as a Lamb who was slain (Revelation 5:1-6:17; Daniel 8:26, 12:4, 9)
- Six of seven seals securing GOD's prophecy/words/decree are opened (Revelation 6:1-17; Daniel 8:26, 12:9)
- 144,000 slaves of GOD are sealed with the mark of GOD (Revelation 7:1-4)
- The seventh seal is opened (Revelation 8:1)
- Five of seven trumpets are blown, setting in motion the destruction of one third of the earth, one third of sea creatures dying, the darkening of one third of light that radiates from the sun, moon and stars, and the torment of people who do not have the seal of GOD on their foreheads. This ends the first woe (Revelation 7:2-4, 8:1-9:12)
- The sixth trumpet is blown and one third of humankind is decreed to be killed by fire, sulfur and smoke (Revelation 9:13-21)
- Seven thunders sound (thunder is biblically associated with the voice of GOD), suggesting the possibility that another mystery might be declared to postpone the end, until a mighty angel announces there will be no more delay (Revelation 10:1; Daniel 12: 9-10)
- For 3 ½ years (42 months), two witnesses dressed in sackcloth (mourning clothes) publicly prophecy against those who dwell on the Earth who are following the beast, and at the conclusion of their testimonies they are killed. While Earth dwellers celebrate, some from among the peoples and tribes and languages and nations refuse to allow

- the two bodies to be buried, in anticipation of prophecy being fulfilled. 3 ½ days later, GOD's breath of life enters the two witnesses and they stand on their feet and are taken up to heaven. Within the hour a great earthquake occurs, killing 7,000 people. <u>This ends the second woe</u> (Revelation 11:1-12)
- The seventh trumpet is blown and the kingdom of the world officially becomes the kingdom of GOD and GOD's Savior. The dragon is cast down to the Earth with its angels and woe is the Earth. The beast is furious because it knows its time is short. <u>This begins the third woe</u> (Revelation 11:15, 12:9-12; <u>Daniel 8:5-8, 9:26a</u>)
- Babylon the great comes under the reign and rule of the first beast, whose number is 666 (let the reader understand). The beast is savage and monstrous in appearance and behavior, offensive, spiteful, vicious, and has a loud, boasting and blasphemous mouth. It seeks to eliminate, destroy and overpower the principled and ethical, and subjugate and suppress different cultures, peoples, nations and races. The beast was once wounded but did not die, and is followed and admired by a great many people who believe it's invincible (Revelation 13:1-10, 18; <u>Daniel 5:1-12, 7:7-8, 23-27)</u>
- A second beast, the false prophet and viceroy of the first beast, makes an idol image of the first beast and gives it the ability to speak (possibly via artificial intelligence). The image commands everyone, great and small, rich and poor, free and slave, to worship it (as though it was GOD), and demands that all people pledge their allegiance by being marked on the right hand or forehead with the name of the first beast or the number of its name. Those refusing to be marked lose the right to buy and sell. (Revelation 13:11-18; <u>Daniel 3:1-30, 9:26b-27)</u>
- 144,000 slaves of GOD are redeemed from humankind as first fruits for GOD and the Lamb (Revelation 14:1-5; <u>Daniel 12:13</u>?)
- The Lord appears in a cloud and reaps the earth (or gathers His people). An angel follows the Lord and reaps the grape harvest of the earth for the great winepress of the wrath of GOD (Revelation 14:14-20; <u>Daniel 7:13-14</u>)

- The seven bowls of GOD's wrath are filled with plagues and given to seven angels, who pour six of the seven bowls out on the Earth and throw the seventh into the air. At the pouring out of the first bowl, painful and contagious sores come on the people who bear the mark of the beast and worship its image. With the emptying of each of the bowls, the time of tribulation worsens. Rather than repent, the people blame GOD for their anguish and torment (Revelation 15:1-8, 16:1-21; Daniel 9:1-19)
- The great city of Babylon falls and there is rejoicing in heaven (Revelation 17:1-19:10)
- The Lord Jesus Christ returns for battle with the armies of heaven and is victorious. The great dragon/Satan/serpent/devil is defeated and imprisoned during the Lord's reign of 1000 years. When the 1000 years are ended, Satan is released and gathers together an army whose number is like the sand of the sea and they march against the camp of the saints (the remnant), but fire comes down from heaven and consumes Satan and its army. Judgement before the throne of GOD begins (Revelation 19:11-20:15; Daniel 7:9-12)
- The New Heaven, a New Earth, and the New Jerusalem come down from heaven (Revelation 21:1-22:5; Daniel 8:13-14)

Outsider

A listener who hears but does not understand what any of it means; 2. An emerging social term for a person living on the outside of prison.

(Isaiah 6:9-10; Mark 4:10-12; John 8:23-27)

Parable

A story-telling method used by GOD and Jesus of Nazareth to communicate with outsiders. Unclear is whether parables were a deliberate "smart as a snake-harmless as a dove" way to ensure confusion among adversaries, or whether parables simply sounded confusing to outsiders because they lacked a shared point or root of origin from which to understand.

(Isaiah 6:8-10; Ezekiel 17:1-16, 24:1-5; Matthew 13:1-16; Mark 4:1-9; Luke 19:11-27)

Peace

> Fears, doubts and distracting noises are gone; 2. When one's soul is satisfied only by GOD.
>
> (Psalm 4:8, 85:8, 119:165; Matthew 6:33; John 14:27, 16:33)

People of the World (Dwellers on the Earth)

> Those on Earth who love the glory that comes from the world more than the glory that comes from GOD; 2. Wandering stars.
>
> (John 8:12-20, 39-47; 17:16; 1 John 2:18-19, 4:1-6; Jude 1:3-16; Revelation 11:10, 13:8)

Peoples, Tribes, Languages and Nations

> Believers and people of faith from among the many peoples, tribes, languages and nations for whom salvation belongs to GOD who sits on the heavenly throne, and to the Lamb; 2. Those receiving white robes.
>
> (Genesis 12:3; Psalm 67:1-7; Isaiah 2:2-4; Daniel 7:13-14; Zechariah 8:20-23; Matthew 28:19-20; John 4:742; Acts 2:5-24, 17:24-32; Colossians 3:1-13; Revelation 5:9-10, 7:9-10, 11:9, 17:15)

Perfection

> The state of faultlessness.
>
> (Matthew 5:48; Philippians 3:12-16; Colossians 1:21-23; Hebrews 10:14-18)

Plague (see Seven Angels with Plagues)

Poor (The)

> People bound together by the shared pain of living without.
>
> (Deuteronomy 15:7-11; 1 John 3:16-17)

Prayer

> An honest desire of the heart, spoken aloud or unspoken, whispered into GOD's invisible ears.
>
> (2 Chronicles 7:14; Mark 11:23-25)

Preach

> To speak as a messenger of the Lord of hosts; 2. The public testimony of what GOD has done, is doing, and is going to do.
>
> (Ezekiel 33:6-7; Malachi 2:1,4-8; Mark 1:38; Acts 8:4; Ephesians 3:8-12, Revelation 1:1, 11:3-11)

Prisoner

> Physical confinement and restraint using walls, water, chains, wires and/or shackles; 2. To be held captive or paralyzed within one's own mind by fears, what ifs, and illusions; 3. The boundaries put in place by someone according to their pre-determined level of effort, comfort and risk.
>
> (Genesis 39:19-23; Judges 16:21-22; 1 Samuel 22:6-19; Zechariah 9:11-12; Mark 5:1-4; John 18:12; Acts 4:32-5:11, 8:3; 2 Timothy 2:3-11)

Progress (Spiritual)

> Determined according to one's growth and advancement in wisdom, understanding and obedience, measured in degrees of depth, height and width rather than the world's measurement systems of educational degrees, labor production equations and fitness technology products; 2. Graduating to a new spiritual level while experiencing fewer and fewer regrets.
>
> (1 Samuel 2:26; Luke 2:52, 8:15; 1 Corinthians 2:6-13; 2 Corinthians 3:18; Ephesians 2:1-10, 3:14-19; Philippians 3:13-15; 2 Timothy 2:14-16; Hebrew 5:12-14; 2 Peter 1:5-8)

Prophecy

> GOD declaring the end from the beginning; 2. Truth fulfilling itself; 3. The secrets of GOD revealed.

(Deuteronomy 18:20-22; Isaiah 46:8-11; Ezekiel 34:1-2, 7; Joel 2:28-29; Amos 3:7-8; Acts 13:26-34; 1 Corinthians 14:1-4; 2 Peter 1:16-21; Revelation 1:1-3)

Prosperity Gospel

>A religious belief system affirming GOD-sanctioned-self-gratification, usually taught to people possessed by unsatisfied longings. The teaching is founded on theology which says the accumulation of material goods is a guaranteed reward for those who give generously to GOD.

>(Malachi 3:6-15; Matthew 6:24, 19:23-24; Mark 10:17-31; 1 Timothy 6:6-10)

Prostitute (The Great)

>The great Babylon, mother of prostitutes and Earth's abominations.

>(Revelation 17:1-18)

>(Note: Prostitution is generally associated with transactional female sexual immorality, where she gives something of value and receives in return something she needs more. In contrast, men tend to prostitute themselves for personal glory and gain.)

>- An angel holding one of the seven bowls of GOD's wrath carries John away in the spirit into a wilderness and shows him the great prostitute who is to be judged, with whom kings and the ordinary people of Earth have committed sexual immorality and become drunk on her wine. John sees the great prostitute sitting on the great beast, which is covered with blasphemous names and has seven heads and ten horns. Her seat on the beast sits across many waters, connecting her to many nations and kingdoms. The great prostitute is dressed in purple and wears a shade of scarlet matching the color of the great beast, and she is adorned with gold, jewels and pearls. In her hand is a golden cup filled with the abominations and impurities associated with her sexual immorality, and written on her forehead is a mysterious name. The prostitute is drunk with the blood of the saints (Revelation 17:1-5).

- An angel holding one of the seven bowls explains to John the mystery of the great prostitute. The waters that the prostitute sits on are peoples, multitudes, nations, and languages. The horns, who are of one mind and collectively hate the prostitute, hand their power to the second beast, who turns on the prostitute and destroys her. (Revelation 17:15-18).

Purpose

To figure out what it means to be you; 2. The mission, service or reason one was called into being by GOD.

(Exodus 9:16; Proverbs 16:4; Ecclesiastes 3:1-8; John 12:27)

Quickly

From a human perspective, a subjective span or speed of time indicating some degree of immediacy or urgency, as in soon or 'now'. From GOD's perspective, quickly can mean a single day or a thousand years.

(1 Samuel 17:17; Psalm 40:17, 70:1; Luke 18:6-8; John 16:16; Acts 22:17-18; 2 Peter 3:8-9; Revelation 3:11, 11:14, 22:7, 12, 20)

Quiet

Stillness in the soul; 2. The absence of fear, anxiety and sound.

(Exodus 14:14; Job 6:24; Psalm 37:7, 131:1-2; Proverbs 29:11; Luke 5:15-16; 2 Timothy 1:7)

Rapture

The word is not found in the Bible, but many use the term to describe the Christian expectation of "meeting the Lord in the air" at His coming on the clouds as King.

(John 14:1-3; Acts 1:6-11; 1 Corinthians 15:51-52; Philippians 3:20-21; 1 Thessalonians 4:16-17; 1 John 3:2-3; Revelation 3:10, 7:4-8, 14:1-5, 19:11-16)

Reborn

> To be born a second time by the power of GOD's Spirit of Truth as a spiritually awakened and aware human being.
>
> (John 1:12-13, 3:3-8; Acts 1:4-5; Ephesians 4:17-24; Colossians 3:1-17; 1 Peter 1:22-24; 1 John 5:1-5)

Reconciled/Reconciliation

> To bridge differences or agree to disagree; 2. To reunite or resign; 3. To sort out or submit; 4. To make peace or mediate terms of peace.
>
> (Genesis 27:41, 32:6-8, 33:1-17; Joshua 24:14-15; 61:1-3; Romans 5:11; 2 Corinthians 5:18-20)

Redemption/Redeemed

> Divine acquittal through faith and belief in Jesus of Nazareth as GOD's promised Messiah; 2. An act of grace on GOD's part whereby an individual's past crimes, sins, convictions and shames are pardoned and they are brought back into right relationship with the Creator.
>
> (Isaiah 43:1, 44: 22; Luke 21:28; John 3:16-17; Colossians 1:11-14; Titus 2:11-14)

Religion

> Theological teachings, doctrines and systems for worshipping GOD; 2. The industrial ecclesiastical complex charged with maintaining social and moral order.
>
> (Matthew 6:1-4; Luke 4:16-20; Acts 5:1-11, 15:1-21; 2 Corinthians 3:1-11; Galatians 5:1-6; Hebrews 9:1-12; James 1:26-27)

Remnant

> A small quantity that remains.
>
> (Genesis 45:4-8; Ezra 9:8; Isaiah 1:9, 10:20-23, 11:16; Jeremiah 23:1-4; Joel 2:30-32; Micah 2:12; Romans 9:27-28, 11:5; Revelation 12:17)

Repent/Repentance

> Loathing for what one has done and grief about the state of one's life, to the extent it leads to a change, or transformation, in one's thinking, speech, actions and behavior.
>
> (Ezekiel 18:30-32, 36:22-23, 31-32; Matthew 4:17; Acts 17:30-34; 2 Corinthians 7:10-11)

Restorative Justice

> The return of what greed and selfishness have consistently and without shame stolen from others.
>
> (Joel 2:25-26; Malachi 3:9-12)

Resurrection

> GOD's non-mechanical, non-industrial, no help needed, miraculously-and-mysteriously-powered-driven restoration of life after death.
>
> (Job 19: 25-27; Dan 12:2-3; Luke 14:14, 24:5-7; John 5:21, 28-89; Romans 8:11; 1 Corinthians 15:12-19; Revelation 20:4-6)

Resurrection (First)

> The first resurrection of the dead. This group includes the 12 individuals who are to judge the twelve tribes of Israel, the people beheaded for delivering the testimony of Jesus and the WORD of GOD, and those who did not worship the beast or its image and did not receive its mark on their foreheads or hands. They are to reign with Yeshua/Jesus the King for one thousand years. Over them the second death has no power.
>
> (Matthew 19:28; James 1:18; Revelation 13:16; 20:4-6)

Resurrection (Second)

> The resurrection of the remaining dead, leading to either eternal life or the second death.
>
> (Daniel 7:9-10, 12:1-2; Matthew 19:29-30; Revelation 20:5a, 12-15)

Revelation (Book of)

> The twenty-seventh and final book in the New Testament; 2. An eschatological or prophetic biblical record of the visions seen and heard by John, a slave of GOD imprisoned on the island of Patmos. The revelation is from Jesus the Christ, who is revealing information from GOD about things soon to take place on the Earth, so that Believers might prepare; 2. For those who are perishing Revelation is a book of terror and warning, but for those who keep the commandments of GOD and hold to the testimony of Jesus, it is one more book in the Bible proclaiming the Good News about GOD's victory over evil. The worst eventually gets better for those who endure, although it seems to take a while, while the wicked and the unrepentant go from bad to worse to disappearing altogether, never to be seen or heard from again. (Revelation 1-22)

Reward

> A gift or honor presented in recognition of faithful service or commendable achievements.
>
> (Jeremiah 17:10; Matthew 10:40-42; 1 Corinthians 9:24; Galatians 6:9; Revelation 22:12)

Righteous

> The state of right-doing, blamelessness, innocence and clean hands in the eyes of GOD.
>
> (Psalms 34:15, 37:28; Proverbs 21:2-3; Ezekiel 18:5; Matthew 5:6; 2 Corinthians 5:21; Philippians 2:14-15; 1 Timothy 4:6-10; 2 Timothy 2:15, 22; Titus 3:4-7; 1 Peter 2:24; 1 John 2:28-29)

Sabbath

> One day of seven ordained by GOD as the day set aside for worship and resting from the burdens and work obligations normally shouldered the other six days of the week.
>
> (Genesis 2:3; Exodus 20:8, Jeremiah 17:24; Luke 4:16, 23:56)

Saints (of GOD)

> The martyrs of Yeshua/Jesus; 2. Holy beings who keep the commandments of GOD and/or the faith of Jesus; 2. The public perception of someone living as holy as they appear to be.
>
> (Psalm 34:9, 85:8; 1 Corinthians 1:2; Revelation 5:8, 6:9-11, 13:7a, 17:6)

Samaritan

> Samaritans trace their origin to the tribes of Ephraim and Manasseh. After Israel's deportation by the Assyrians, some Israelites left behind intermarried with foreign settlers. They are seen as 'half-breeds' by Jews returning to Israel to rebuild the temple, after being liberated from captivity by king Cyrus of Persia.
>
> (Genesis 48:14-20; 2 Kings 17:24-29; Ezra 2:1; Luke 10:25-32)

Sanctuary

> The physical or mental space where the presence of GOD is experienced most intimately.
>
> (Exodus 25:1-9; Psalm 73:16-17; Ezekiel 11:16; 1 Corinthians 6:19; 1 Peter 2:4-5)

Sarai/Sarah

> Abraham's wife, who laughed at the thought of GOD doing the impossible; 2. Mother of Isaac.
>
> (Genesis 18:9-15, 21:1-7)

Satan

> The enemy of GOD and Believers; 2. The deceiver of the world and inventor of temptations, life-threatening circumstances, day-to-day obstacles, frustrations and lies; 3. The Beast at war with all who keep the commandments of GOD and hold to the testimony Jesus.
>
> (1 Chronicles 21:1; Isaiah 14:12-14; Matthew 16:23; 1 Thessalonians 2:17-18; 2 Thessalonians 2:9; Ephesians 6:12; 1 Peter 5:8, Revelations 12:17)

Savior (GOD's)

> Yeshua/Jesus of Nazareth; 2. The image of the invisible GOD; 3. The firstborn of all creation; 4. Someone who saves, rescues and delivers another from danger and death.
>
> (2 Kings 13:5; Isaiah 7:14, 44:6-8; Matthew 1:18-25; Luke 1:26-31, 2:11-12, 16-17, 21; John 1:29-31, 11:25-27, 12:47; Acts 4:11-12; Colossians 1:11-20; Hebrews 2:14-18; 1 John 4:14; Revelation 1:8)

Saved/Salvation

> Delivered, or saved, from experiencing the Second Death, the state of eternal separation from GOD.
>
> (John 3:16-17, 36, 5:28-29; Romans 6:9-11, 23, 10:13; Ephesians 2:4-5; 1 Thessalonians 5:9-10; Revelation 3:5, 20:4-6)

Seal/Sealed

> An instrument (ring, cartridge seal, stone, etc.) used to mark an object for the purpose of ownership identification; 2. A mark signifying the seal of assurance that the contents inside have not been changed; 3. GOD's mark on the forehead of the 144,000 slaves who stand under GOD's protection; 4. The name or mark received on the forehead or right hand of those on Earth who follow the beast; 5. Marks and seals were used in ancient times to enforce empire mandates (i.e. Ptolemy IV, ruler of Egypt 221-205 BCE, required Jewish individuals within his realm to be marked or branded with an ivy leaf, the symbol of the god Dionysus).
>
> (Genesis 4:15; Exodus 28:21, 36, 39:14; Nehemiah 9:38; Isaiah 44:5; Jeremiah 32:10; Ezekiel 9:3-4; Daniel 6:17, 8:26, 12:4; Zechariah 3:1-2; Matthew 27:65-66; John 6:27; Ephesians 1:13-14; 2 Timothy 2:19; Revelation 7:3-4, 9:4, 13:16-17)

Second Coming of Jesus as King/Coming of the Lord/The Day of the Lord

> The second coming of Jesus as conquering King, the day and time unknown except to GOD; 2. The storm of the Lord.
>
> (Jeremiah 30:23-24; Daniel 7:13-14; Amos 5:18-20; Matthew 24:29-31, 36-42; Mark 13:24-27, 32-37; Luke 12:35-40, 21:25-28,

34-36; John 5:25-27; Hebrew 9:24-28; Revelation 1:4-7, 3:3, 14:14-16, 22:12-17, 20)

Second Death

Eternal death.

(Revelation 20:6, 14)

Self-Control

Internalized self-discipline.

(Proverbs 18:21, 25:28, 29:11; 1 Corinthians 9:25-27; Galatians 5:24; 1 Thessalonians 4:4; Titus 1:8, 2:11-12)

Separation

The act of separating created things from the presence of GOD or into distinct kinds, groupings, categories, ranks, types, and order.

(Genesis 1:3-27, 3:22-24; Leviticus 20:24b-26; Numbers 8:14; Ezra 10:10-11; Isaiah 59:1-2; Jeremiah 3:1; Matthew 19:3-6, 20:20-28, 25:31-34, 41; Mark 10:10-12, 42-45; Romans 8:38-39; 1 Corinthians 7:15; 2 Corinthians 14-18; Ephesians 2: 11-12; 2 Thessalonians 1:5-10; Titus 3: 10; James 4:4; Revelation 21:6-8)

Servant (GOD's)

Biblically associated with greatness; 2. One who voluntarily agrees to serve a master or lord in exchange for compensation or the expectation of reward; 3. A hired hand; 4. Ministers of righteousness.

(Leviticus 25:6, 39-43; 55; Psalm 116:16; Matthew 20:26-27; Luke 15:17-19, 22:24-27; 2 Corinthians 11:15)

(Note: The New Testament differentiates between servant (Gr. *diakonos*) and slave (*doulos*). The servant is great, but the slave is first in rank—Matthew 20:25-28)

Set His/My/Your Face Toward…

Bound and determined; 2. The firm resolve to carry out a matter.

(Ezekiel 21:2; Daniel 9:3, 11:17a; Matthew 20:17-19; Luke 9:51)

Seven (the Number)

> Representing the oneness of the seven spirits of GOD and the unity of GOD's promises throughout all ages; 2. Symbolizing completion or perfection; 3. A prime number whose factors are 1 and itself (7); 4. A means by which to authenticate and certify a power as belonging to, or a message as originating from, the One Holy GOD.
>
> (Genesis 2:1-3, 7:1-5; Leviticus 25:4a; Numbers 8:1-3; Deuteronomy 6:4; Psalm 12:6; Zechariah 3:9-10, 4:10; Mark 12:29; Revelation 1:4, 12, 16, 19-20, 4:5, 5:6)

[Seven as organized in the Book of Revelation]

Seven Golden Lampstands

> Seven heavenly lampstands are representative of seven churches on earth, or the Church in its fullness, seven symbolizing oneness and completion. In John's vision, he hears someone speaking. He turns around to see who it is and sees one like a s/Son of man dressed in a long robe with a golden sash tied around His chest, hair the color of wool, eyes like flames of fire, and feet like burnished bronze. The Son of Man speaks with a loud voice, has a sharp two-edged sword in His mouth and is standing in the midst of seven lampstands; 2. A lampstand elevates and supports a lamp to allow for better light distribution, enabling others to see; 3. The Menorah (Hebrew for lamp) used in the ancient temple in Jerusalem had seven candles, symbolizing GOD's spiritual presence.
>
> (Revelation 1:12-13, 20, 2:1, 5; Exodus 25:31, 37; Number 8:1-4; 1 Kings 7:48-49; 2 Chronicles 4:7; Joel 2:27; Daniel 5:5; Zephaniah 3:17; Zechariah 4:1-2; Matthew 5:14-16; Mark 4:21-23; Luke 8:16-18; John 12:35-36; Colossians 1:15-18; Hebrews 4:11-13, 9:1-2)

Seven Stars

> Seven stars represent the seven angels (human or divine) supervising the seven churches. Each angel is responsible for ensuring the content of the letter each receives is read aloud to the church under its care.
>
> (Revelation 1:8, 16-20, 2:1, 8, 12, 18, 3:1, 7, 14)

Seven Letters to Seven Churches

GOD has a WORD/a testimony to share with the slaves of GOD on Earth, so that they're informed and understand the things that are about to soon happen, so that they won't fear or think GOD has forgotten them. GOD gives the WORD to Yeshua/Jesus the Christ, who reveals it to His own angel (the Spirit) who delivers the WORD to John through a series of visions. Obediently, John bears witness to the WORD of GOD and the testimony of Jesus Christ by describing in writing all that he sees and hears, but his first task is to write seven letters to seven angels (human or divine) who are responsible for guiding seven churches. The letters find their way to the churches, identified as Ephesus, Smyrna, Pergamum, Thyatira, Sardis, Philadelphia and Laodicea. The seven churches are believed to have existed along a semicircular route in Asia Province (i.e. Thyatira was located on the road leading from Pergamum to Sardis, which was 80 miles east of Smyrna, etc.); 2. The term <u>seven churches</u> may also allude to the complete history of the institutionalized Church from beginning to end (roughly 1st or 2nd C. E. to the present), with the number seven symbolizing completion and oneness. The content and context described in each of the seven letters is different, but all of the churches are warned to pay attention to what's also being said to the other six.

(Revelation 1:4, 10-11, 2:1-3:22; Luke 24:49; John 14:15-17, 15:26, 16:7-11; Acts 1:6-8, 2:1-4, 10:44-45, 131:13-23; 2 Peter 3:8-10)

- The angel overseeing the church in **Ephesus** delivers a message from One who holds seven stars in His right hand and walks in the midst of seven golden lampstands. The church is commended for patiently enduring, not growing weary, and for hating evil. The complaint against them is that they no longer love the Lord as deeply as they once did. The church has fallen away. If it does not repent its lampstand will be removed (the church will cease to exist), but the one (in the church) who endures to the end will eat from the Tree of Life in the paradise of GOD. (Revelation 1:13, 2:1-7; Genesis 3:22-24; Joel 2:27; Zephaniah 3:17; Matthew 18:20; 1 Corinthians 9:24-27; 2 Peter 2:20-22;)

- The angel overseeing the church in **Smyrna** delivers a message from One who is called the first and last, who died and came to life again. The church is assured the Lord sees and understands how dire their situation is and knows they are contending with people who claim and pretend to be Jews (or of Judah) but are not, and a word of encouragement is given. The church sees itself as poor but in the eyes of the Lord, it are rich. The church is encouraged not to be afraid of what is coming and told what Satan is preparing to do next. The promise made to the one faithful unto death is that they will not be harmed by the second death and will receive the crown of life. (Revelation 2:8-11, 20:6, 14, 21:8; Malachi 4:1; Matthew 10:16-22, 24-28; John 3:16, 8:31-38, 11:25-26, 12:49-50, 16:33; Romans 8:18; 1 Corinthians 9:24-27; 2 Timothy 4:8; Hebrews 9:24-28; James 1:12)

- The angel overseeing the church in **Pergamum** delivers a message from One who has the sharp two-edged sword, one side to defend, the other to defeat. The Lord knows and understands that they are enduring hardship in the very center of evil, where Satan has its throne. The church is commended for holding fast to the Lord's name, and for not letting go of their faith in Him or denying Him, but the complaint against them is that some among them are condoning the teachings of Balaam, who claimed to know the mind of GOD and taught the king of Moab what to do to cause the sons of Israel to stumble and fall into sin. Others in the church have seemingly perverted the teachings of Nicolaus, one of seven men chosen to serve as a deacon in the early church in Jerusalem, by acting like lords and teaching that separation from the world is not required for Believers. The church has fallen away. If it does not repent, the Lord will make war against them with the sword of His mouth, but the one who endures and conquers will receive some of the hidden manna and a white stone with a new name written on it, which only the receiver and the giver will know. (Revelation 1:16, 2:12-17; Exodus 16:4, 13-15, 31; Numbers 11:7, 22-24; Joshua 4:19-24, 5:10-12; Psalm 118:22; Nehemiah 9:20-21; Matthew 18:1-4, 20:25-28; Mark 10:42-45; Luke 22:24-

27; John 6:28-33, 47-51, Acts 6:5; Romans 16:17-18; 2 Timothy 3:1-7; Titus 3:10; Hebrews 4:12-13; 1 Peter 2:4-5; 2 John 9-11)

- The angel overseeing the church in **Thyatira** delivers a message from the Son of GOD who has eyes like flames of fire and feet like burnished bronze. The Lord knows the church's history of good works, love, faith, service and patience. The complaint against them is that they are tolerating a wicked, immoral and unrepentant woman who is attempting to bring pagan worship into the kingdom of GOD, as Jezebel did, and teaching the sons of GOD to practice sexual immorality and eat food sacrificed to idol (false) gods. The time allotted for the wicked woman to repent has passed, her judgment declared. Any one committing adultery (unfaithfulness) with her will experience the great tribulation and the second death, unless they repent, and each person will receive the reward their works deserve. Those who do not accept or go along with the wicked woman's teachings are to hold fast to their faith until the Son of GOD comes again. If they endure to the end and conquer, they will be granted authority to rule over the nations and receive the morning star (Revelation 1:14, 2:18-29, 20:4, 21:8, 22:16; 1 Kings 18:1-4, 20-40, 19:1-2, 21:1-16; 2 Kings 9:30-37; Matthew 24:21-22; John 3:16-21, 10:34-36, 11:4, 19:7, 20:30-31; 1 Corinthians 15:41)

- The angel overseeing the church in **Sardis** delivers a message from Him who has the seven spirits of GOD and the seven stars. The Lord says that while the church has a reputation for being alive, it's dead. They must wake up and strengthen what little faith they have left, which is about to die, because in the eyes of GOD their works are incomplete. The church has fallen away, and only a few people have not soiled their garments (compromised their faith). If they do not repent, the Lord will come like a thief in the night against them. The one who conquers to the end will be clothed in a white garment and walk with the Lord, because they are deemed worthy. Their name will never be removed from the book of life and the Lord will come to their defense before His Father and the angels. (Revelation

1:4, 16, 3:1-6, 5:6, 16:15, 20:12-14, 15; Matthew 5:48, 24:36-44; 1 Thessalonians 5:1-6)

- The angel overseeing the church in **Philadelphia** delivers a message from the Holy One, the true one who has the key of David and can open what no one can shut, and shut what no one can open. The Lord knows the church's works and that it has very little power in the world, but He commends it for keeping the Lord's word and not denying their allegiance to Him. Those belonging to the Lord are assured that those belonging to the synagogue of Satan (who say they are Believers but are not), will soon bow down to them, the faithful ones, and they are encouraged to hold fast to their faith so that no one can take their crown. The one who conquers, who keeps the WORD of the Lord about patient endurance to the end, is to be kept from the hour of trial coming on the whole world and will become a mainstay in GOD's temple, never to leave again. Written on them will be GOD's name, the name of the new city of GOD, and the Lord's own name.
(Revelation 3:7-13, 15:1-16:21, 19:11-12; Genesis 31:13; Exodus 24:4; Deuteronomy 31:15; 1 Samuel 2:8; Isaiah 22:22; Galatians 2:9)

- The angel overseeing the church in **Laodicea** delivers a message from the Amen, the faithful and true witness, the beginning of GOD's creation. The Lord knows the church's works. They are neither cold nor hot—they are lukewarm, indifferent, apathetic, half-hearted, uninterested, undecided, uncertain and doubtful. The church believes itself to be rich, but in the Lord's eyes it is woeful, deplorable, poor, blind and naked. The church is warned to buy gold, white robes and eye medicine from the Lord, so that they can become rich, cover the shame of their nakedness and see. Those whom the Lord loves, He will reprove and discipline. The final invitation to hear what the spirit is saying to the church and let GOD into their heart is given. The one who endures and conquers is granted the right to sit beside the Lord on His throne, as the Lord conquered and sits beside His Father's throne.
(Revelation 3:14-22, 13:1-18, 19:11; Genesis 1:1-2, Psalm 94:12, 110:1, 118:17-18; Proverbs 3:11-12; Jeremiah

30:11; Matthew 22:41-46; Luke 9:57-62; John 1:1-5, 19:30; Acts 2:29-36; Hebrews 1:1-5, 13-14; 12:3-6)

Seven Spirits of the One GOD

> The all-seeing, all-hearing and all-knowing Living GOD, seven symbolizing oneness and completion.
>
> (Revelation 1:4, 3:1, 4:5; 5:6; Deuteronomy 6:4; Joshua 3:10; 2 Chronicles 16:9a; Job 28:23-24, Psalm 147:5; Isaiah 11:1-2, 44:6; Jeremiah 10:10, 23:24; Daniel 6:25-26; Zechariah 3:6-9, 4:10; John 17:3; 1 Corinthians 8:5-6; Hebrews 4:11-13; 1 John 4:1)

Seven Seals

> One seated on the heavenly throne holds a scroll with writing on the front and back. The scroll is sealed with seven seals and contains the prophecies concerning the order of things to come. No one in heaven or on earth knows what the prophecies say because no one in heaven, on earth, or under the earth has been worthy or righteous enough to open the seals and read the written words. Not until Yeshua/Jesus of Nazareth, the Lion of the tribe of Judah, the Root of David sent into the world by GOD, appears. Jesus endures to the end of His life and conquers death. He, alone, is worthy to unseal and read the scroll. John describes Him as a Lamb with seven horns and seven eyes, the seven spirits of GOD sent out into all the earth. When the Lamb takes the scroll from the right hand of the One seated on the throne, the four living creatures and twenty-four elders fall down before the Lamb singing a new song, and all of heaven celebrates.
>
> (Revelation 4:1-5:14; John 1:1-4, 9-14, 19:28-20:1, 11-18; Luke 23:46-47, 24:1-12; Mark 15:34-37, 16:1-8; Matthew 27:46-50, 28:1-10)
>
> - The opening of the <u>first seal</u> reveals the assurance of victory. (Revelation 1:16, 3:12, 6:1-2, 19:11-16)
>
> - The opening of the <u>second seal</u> reveals violence and war steadily replacing and overcoming peace on Earth. (Revelation 6:3-4)

- The opening of the <u>third seal</u> reveals a world where the wealthy continually indulge themselves while the poor pay a day's labor for a loaf of bread. (Revelation 6:5-6)

- The opening of the <u>fourth seal</u> reveals the limits imposed by GOD on Death's authority and ability to destroy by violence. (Revelation 6:7-8)

- The opening of the <u>fifth seal</u> is a word of comfort and assurance to those killed for upholding the word of GOD and bearing witness about the Son of GOD. (Revelation 6:9-11)

- The opening of the <u>sixth seal</u> produces a great earthquake, the sun turns black, a full moon turns the color of blood, and the stars in heaven fall to the Earth. The events are destructive enough that everyone, rich and poor, imprisoned and free, recognize the moment for what it is. The great day of the coming wrath of GOD and the Lamb has arrived. (Revelation 6:12-17)

- The opening of the <u>seventh seal</u> produces a silence in heaven lasting about a half-hour (comparable to the calm in the eye of a hurricane?). (Revelation 8:1)

Seven Angels with Seven Trumpets

Seven angels are given seven trumpets. A golden censer (a container or vessel used for burning incense) is filled with fire from the alter in heaven and thrown down on the Earth, triggering thunder, rumblings, flashes of lightening and an earthquake. The seven angels prepare to blow their trumpets. The blowing of trumpets (in the Bible) signifies an alarm, calls people to assemble, commands them to march, or is a warning to those about to perish. Four angels, having received power and authority to harm the earth, sea and trees, are constrained from doing their work until all the slaves of GOD have been marked with GOD's seal.

(Revelation 7:1-3, 8:2-9:21, 11:15-19; Exodus 19:16, 19, 20:18-19; Joshua 6:4-20; Isaiah 27:12-13, Joel 2:1)

- When the <u>first trumpet</u> sounds, one-third of the earth is destroyed, impacting the migratory patterns of all living creatures. (Revelation 8:7)
- When the <u>second trumpet</u> sounds, one-third of the sea becomes as undrinkable as blood, with all the natural consequences that follow. (Revelation 8:8-9)
- When the <u>third trumpet</u> sounds, another one-third of Earth's waters are poisoned, and the toxicity level causes many people to die. (Revelation 8:10-11, 12:7-9)
- When the <u>fourth trumpet</u> sounds, one-third of the light from the sun, the moon and the stars is kept from shining. With the blowing of the fifth trumpet, a series of three "Woes" begins. (Revelation 8:12-13)
- When the <u>fifth trumpet</u> sounds, the sun and air are darkened by smoke, and locusts emerge to inflict harm on people who do not have the seal of GOD on their forehead, who are tormented for 5 months but not allowed to die. This concludes the first of three woes. (Revelation 7:3-4, 9:1-12)
- When the <u>sixth trumpet</u> sounds, the four angels prepared for that exact hour, day, month and year are released to kill a third of humankind by means of fire, smoke and sulfur. Humans not killed by these three plagues still do not repent of their evil works. (Revelation 9:13-21)
- When the <u>seventh trumpet</u> sounds, the mystery of GOD is finished. All of heaven is abuzz with the news that the kingdom of the world is now the kingdom of GOD and GOD's Savior, no matter what life looks like on Earth. (Revelation 11:15-19)

Seven Thunders

John sees a mighty angel come down from heaven wrapped in a cloud with a rainbow over His head. His face is as bright as the sun and his legs are like pillars of fire. In His hand is a small open scroll, indicating the contents are not sealed. John hears an angel call out with a loud voice, which sounds to him like thunder (in the Bible, thunder is often associated with GOD's voice). He prepares to write down what the thunder has said, but then hears a voice from heaven telling him *not* to write down what he has heard, ensuring what was said would not come to pass. The thunder may have been the announcing of yet another mystery, a means by which to delay the end for a little while longer, but the angel raises its right hand to heaven and swears by all that is holy there will be no more delay. The children of GOD have suffered long enough.

(Revelation 4:3, 10:1-11, 14:14; Exodus 19:16-19; Job 37:4-5, 40:9; Psalm 29:3-4; John 12:27-29; Hebrew 12:18-19)

Seven Angels with Seven Plagues

Seven angels clothed in pure bright linen with golden sashes around their chests receive a golden bowl full of GOD's wrath. Each angel pours out a bowl of wrath onto the Earth in turn, manifested as plagues. After the pouring of the seventh bowl, the wrath of GOD is finished. Plagues, frequently mentioned throughout the Bible, represent torment, affliction and destruction. During the pouring of bowls, and until the plagues are finished, no heavenly beings are permitted to enter GOD's sanctuary. GOD's face is decidedly set toward the end and no one—not even the one found worthy to open the seven seals—will be able to change GOD's mind.

(Revelation 15:1-8; Genesis 12:17, Exodus 7:17-21, 8:16-19, 9:8-12; Leviticus 26:21-22; Numbers 21:4-7; 1 Samuel 4:8; Jeremiah 14:11-12; Luke 7:21)

Seven Bowls of GOD's Wrath

Seven golden bowls containing the sum total of GOD's rage and indignation, to be poured out on the Earth in the form of plagues, GOD's long-suffering response to the mistreatment, abuse, violence, suffering and killings endured by the saints, prophets and children of GOD, and the fulfillment of the promise to punish those who would not listen and obey.

(Revelation 16:1-21; Genesis 19:1-38; Exodus 32:7-10; Joel 2:30-32; Micah 5:15; Nahum 1:2; Psalm 2:1-6, 7:11-13, 14:1; Isaiah 34:1-2, 59:1-2; Jeremiah 21:11-14, 30:23; Ezekiel 8:16-18, 22:17-22; Daniel 12:1-2; Matthew 13:36-43, 23:34-36, 24:20-22; John 3:16, 36; Acts 17:30-31; Romans 1:18-21, 2:1-5, 12:19; Ephesians 5:6; 2 Thessalonians 1:5-9; Hebrews 10:31, 12:25-29; 2 Peter 3:9)

- The pouring of the <u>first bowl</u> results in painful sores on the bodies of people sealed with the mark of the beast (Revelation 13:16-17, 16:1-2)
- The pouring of the <u>second bowl</u> causes every living thing in the sea to die, significantly impacting the food supply (Revelation 16:3)
- The pouring of the <u>third bowl</u> causes rivers and springs to become unfit to drink (Revelation 16:4-7)
- The pouring of the <u>fourth bowl</u> causes those sealed with the mark of the beast to burn and blister from the scorching heat of the sun. Rather than repent of their wrongdoing, they curse GOD (Revelation 16:8-9)
- The <u>fifth bowl</u> is poured out on the throne of the beast and the Earth goes dark, all hope is gone. Rather than repent of their wrongdoing, the people curse and blame GOD for their pain, sores and anguish (Revelation 16:10-11)
- The pouring of the <u>sixth bowl</u> causes the great river Euphrates to dry up (this is on the eastern border of the inheritance given to the offspring of Abraham). The absence of water eliminates a major defensive barrier protecting Israel, and provides an avenue of escape for any remnant of GOD's people who remain in Jerusalem (Revelation 16:12-16; Genesis 2:10-14, 15:18; Deuteronomy 1:7, 11:24; Joshua 1:3-4; Isaiah 11:15-16; Matthew 24:15-22)
- The contents of the <u>seventh bowl</u> are tossed into the air, triggering lightening, thunder, hail and a great earthquake on a scale never before see or experienced on earth. Cities and nations fall. The great city of Babylon is remembered by GOD and receives the fury of GOD's wrath. Hailstones weighing one hundred pounds each fall from heaven on people, and they curse GOD for the plague of the hail because it's so severe (Revelation 16:17-21).

Seventh Day

The day blessed and set apart for worshipping GOD and resting.

(Genesis 2:1-3; Exodus 20:8-11; Leviticus 23:3; Deuteronomy 5:12-15; Isaiah 58:13-14; Ezekiel 20:18-21a 24; Matthew 12:1-12; Mark 2:27-28; Luke 6:3-5, 13:10-17, 14:1-6; Hebrew 4:9-10)

Seven Weeks of Years

Forty-nine years.

(Leviticus 25:8)

Seventy (70) Weeks

The period of time appointed, or set aside, by GOD to forgive Israel's transgressions, put an end to the power of sin, atone for iniquity, clear the way for righteousness, seal the visions, prophets and saints, and anoint a holy place for the New Jerusalem. The seventy weeks is divided into time periods of seven weeks (beginning approx. 538 BCE), sixty-two weeks, and one week. In the final (70th) week, a strongman overtakes the city of Jerusalem and makes a covenant of agreement with the people. Halfway through the week (3 ½ years), the strongman breaks the covenant and destroys the city. The decreed end-time plagues and tribulation immediately follow.

(Ezra 1:1-3, 2:1; Jeremiah 25:11-12; Daniel 8:13-14, 9:1-2, 24-27, 12:1-13; Matthew 24:15; Acts 17:26-27)

Shepherd (see Keeper)

Shrewdness

Wisdom according to the world; 2. A worldly principle setting forth the notion that how one attains something is of far less importance than whether or not it was attained through a good deal favorable to one's self.

(Genesis 3:1; Matthew 10:16; Luke 16:1-8)

Sin

The offspring of evil mating with human emotions, desires, thoughts, weaknesses, and worldly belief systems.

(Leviticus 4:1-5:6; Mark 7:14-23; 1 Corinthians 10:1-14; Galatians 5:16-21; James 4:1-17; 1 John 5:16-18)

Sins (of the Antichrist/Dragon/Hasatan/Satan)

> Attempting to unseat GOD and place itself on the heavenly throne, not accepting submission, and shattering the power of the holy people.
>
> (Genesis 2:15-17, 3:1-7; 1 Chronicles 21:1; Isaiah 14:12-14; Ezekiel 28:1-10; Daniel 8:8-12, 12:3-4a; Zechariah 3:1-2; John 12:31-32, 14:30; 2 Corinthians 4:2-6; Ephesians 6:12; 2 Thessalonians 2:3-10; Revelation 12:7-9, 13:7a)

Sins (of Israel)

> Sexual idolatry and immorality (men began taking their sisters as wives), sacrificing children, idol worship, repeated disobedience, and breaking the covenant with GOD.
>
> (Genesis 6:1-3, 5-8; Judges 2:11-15, 4:1, 6:1; 1 Kings 16:29-33; 2 Kings 17:1-2, 21:1-6; Nehemiah 9:1-38; Isaiah 1:2-4; Jeremiah 2:1-13, 3:6; Ezekiel 16:1-63; 17:11-15, 20:1-32; Hosea 4:1-2, 11:1-7; Amos 5:18-24; Micah 1:1-7; John 8:31-47; Romans 9:1-29)

Slave (of GOD)

> Biblically associated with the rank of First; 2. One whose duty is to serve GOD of their own free will, without expectation of reward.
>
> (Deuteronomy 23:15; Matthew 20:1-28; Luke 22:24-27; 1 Corinthians 7:21-23; Revelation 1:1, 7:3-4)
>
> (Note: The Greek word used in the New Testament scriptures above is slave (*doulos*), not servant (*diakonos*), signifying differences in eternal ranking. The servant is great, but the slave is first)

Smart as a Snake and Harmless as a Dove

> Sophisticated shrewdness working in full cooperation with the commands of GOD and Jesus; 2. Recognizing when someone is trying to deflect, misdirect or otherwise deceive, and thinking quickly on one's feet to make decisions and respond appropriately and righteously.
>
> (Genesis 3:1; Hosea 7:11; Matthew 7:15, 10:16; Romans 16:17-19; 2 Corinthians 11:1-3; Philippians 2:15)

Sober Minded

>The state of being composed and steady enough to refuse any kind of intoxicant that might rob one of either sanity or sound judgment; 2. To be watchful, awake and led in a straight way.
>
>(Isaiah 5:11-12; 1 Corinthians 15:34; 1 Thessalonians 5:6; 1 Peter 4:7, 5:8)

Son of m/Man

>A term meant to emphasize a human in the flesh, in contrast to their divine nature (i.e. Son of GOD).
>
>(Numbers 23:19; Ezekiel 11:14, 20:2, 27; Daniel 7:13-14; Matthew 9:6-7, 17:22-23; Mark 14:62; Luke 19:10)

Speech

>The spoken word blended with tone of voice and style of delivery.
>
>(Psalm 19:14, 37:30, Proverbs 15:1-2; Ecclesiastes 9:17; Luke 6:45; Ephesians 4:29; Colossians 4:6; James 3:9-10)

Spirit (Holy)

>The Spirit of Truth; 2. The spirit of the LORD; 3. Jesus' promised teacher and interpreter of truth, holiness and righteousness; 4. The divine revealer of things to come.
>
>(Isaiah 11:1-5, 42:1; Joel 2:28-29; Zechariah 4:6-7; John 14:25-26, 16:12-14; Acts 1:8, 2:1-4; Revelation 1:1, 2:7, 11, 17, 29, 3:6, 13, 22)

Spiritual Blindness

>The inability to see truth hiding in plain sight.
>
>(Deuteronomy 29:1-4; Isaiah 43:8; Matthew 15:14; John 9:39-41, 12:36b-40; Ephesians 5:6-10; Corinthians 2:14; 2 Corinthians 4:3-4; Revelation 3:17)

Spiritual Warfare

>The battle against spiritual forces of evil.
>
>(Deuteronomy 28:7-10; Psalm 37:12-17; Isaiah 54:17; Daniel 10:12-13, 21; 2 Corinthians 10:3-5; Ephesians 6:10-18; 1 Timothy 6:11-12; Revelation 12:7-9)

Stars

>GOD's celestial army of angels; 2. Created to give light on the earth, separate light from darkness, serve as signs in the heavens, and identify seasons.
>
>(Genesis 1:14-19; Joshua 5:14a; Psalm 147:4; Isaiah 40:26; Matthew 2:1-2, 24:29; 1 Corinthians 15:41; Jude 1:14-15; Revelation 1:20, 6:12-13)

Steadfast

>Holding firm and following through no matter what; 2. To be tested to the limit and not be crushed or destroyed; 3. Taking one step and day at a time; 4. The path leading to conquering and overcoming; 5. The strength undergirding endurance.
>
>(Psalm 112:7; Isaiah 40:30-31; Matthew 24:13; James 1:12; Revelation 3:11b, 17b,26, 5, 12a, 21)

Study

>The proper response to understanding that a restored relationship with GOD and the gift of salvation are no excuse for neglecting serious theological brainwork; 2. The process by which to better understand and make sense of the inconsistencies between one's life and GOD's promises.
>
>(Psalm 1:1-2; Proverbs 9:9, 18:15; Ecclesiastes 7:25; Luke 2:46-47; 2 Timothy 2:15; 1 Peter 1:10-11, 3:15-16)

Stumbling Block

>A behavior or attitude creating an intentional or unintentional obstacle, barrier, complication, disadvantage, setback, inconvenience, limitation or delay for another.

(Isaiah 8:14-15, 57:14; Matthew 16:21-23; 18:7; Romans 9:30-33, 14:13; 1 Corinthians 8:9)

Surrender

>To be done trying; 2. To concede defeat.

>(Jeremiah 10: 23; Mark 8:34, 14:35-36; Luke 1:38, 9:23, 23:46; Galatians 2:20; James 4:7, 10)

Temptation

>The prelude to sin.

>(Matthew 4:1-11, 26:40-41; 1 Corinthians 10:13; 2 Corinthians 2:10-11; Ephesians 4:26-27; 1 Timothy 6:9-10; Hebrew 2:14-18; James 1:13-15)

Test

>A tool used to assess, measure and provide evidence of personal growth, faithfulness, willingness, allegiance, obedience, humility, etc.

>(Genesis 22:1-18; 2 Chronicles 32:31; Psalm 11:4-5, 26:2; John 6:5-6; Romans 12:2; 1 Thessalonians 5:21; James 1:2-3; 1 John 4:1)

Times of the End/End of Time

>Terms used to refer to the final events of history. Designated as time, times and half a time; end times; end of day; end of the ages; last days. The end represents the conclusion of Genesis' opening verse, "In the beginning…" For the sake of the elect, the number of end days is reduced from 1290 to 1260.

>(Psalm 46:8-9; Ecclesiastes 3:11; Isaiah 10:23, 46:8-11; Ezekiel 7:1-13; Daniel 9:24-27, 12:1-2, 11-13; Matthew 24:3-13, 22, 42; Luke 21:25-28, 31, 34-36; 2 Corinthians 11:12-15; 2 Timothy 3:1-5; 2 Peter 3:1-10; 1 John 2:18; Revelation 1:8, 2:26-29, 8:15, 12:6, 13:5, 21:5-8, 22:12-15)

Tithe

>The voluntary giving of one tenth (1/10) of one's annual earnings, goods or produce.

(Numbers 18:21; Deuteronomy 14:22-29; 2 Chronicles 31:5b-6; Proverbs 3:9-10; Malachi 3:10; Matthew 23:23; Luke 21:1-4; 2 Corinthians 9:6-7; 1 John 3:16-17)

Tongue

    A flexible body part used as an instrument to praise and bless, or as a weapon to disparage, injure, curse and condemn.

    (Psalm 12:3-4, 34:13; Proverbs 18:21; Matthew 12:36-37; James 3:5-10)

Transgression

    Wrong doing and sin.

    (Proverbs 6:16-19; Isaiah 43:25-26; Daniel 9:24; Galatians 5:19-21; Hebrews 10:26-27)

Tribulation

    A time of trouble, distress and suffering, signifying the end of days. The term is often associated with the great tribulation spoken of in Matthew 24:21 and the great trouble mentioned in Daniel 12:1. The troubling times increase in severity such as the earth has never seen before, until the power and authority given by Jesus to the holy people has been completely suppressed and shattered.

    (Deuteronomy 4:30-31; Judges 10:6-9; Jeremiah 30:4-7; Daniel 9:24-27, 12:1-8; Matthew 9:3-8; 13:21, 24:15-16, 21-22, 28:18-20, 29-31, 25:31-46; Mark 13:14-20; Luke 10:19-20; John 16:33; Romans 12:12; Revelation 6:12-17, 7:13-14; 13:10, 15-17, 15:1; 16:1)

Trinity

    A term used by Christians to describe the mystery of the three-person divine household of GOD the Father, Jesus/Yeshua the Son, and the Holy Spirit. Wisdom is represented in the Holy Spirit. In Hebrew and in Greek, the word for spirit is feminine; 2. GOD, three persons in one.

    (Genesis 1:26a; Proverbs 3:13-18, 4:5-9; Isaiah 48:16; Matthew 3:16-17, 28:18-20; Luke 1:35; John 14:26, 15:26; 2 Corinthians 13:14; Revelation 12:1-2)

Truly, Truly

> The equivalent of "I faithfully, legally, sincerely, in fact and reality declare that what I'm saying to you is true and accurate."
>
> (Psalm 119:151-152; John 1:51, 3:3, 5:24, 6:47, 12:24; 14:12, 16:20, etc.; Revelation 21:5)

Truth

> That which actually is or was, which may be unrecognized but cannot be changed; 2. The correct response and rebuttal to all illusions, delusions, shadows, tricks, lies, nightmares, virtual realities and figments of the imagination, without distinction; 3. How things are, rather than how one thought it would be.
>
> (1 Kings 17:24; Psalm 15:2, 86:11; Proverbs 12:22; Daniel 10:21; Matthew 5:18; John 5:24, 16:13; 2 Timothy 2:15)

Trust in God

> Absolute confidence in GOD; 2. Sureness and certainty regarding GOD's abilities to act, which proportionately increases or decreases as doubt and confidence rise or fall.
>
> (Psalm 9:9-10, 56:3-4, 112:7; Isaiah 26:3; Mark 9:24; 1 John 5:14)

Twelve Thrones

> The twelve thrones designated for twelve individuals who are to judge Israel. They come to life during the first resurrection and reign with Yeshua/Jesus for a thousand years. (Also reigning with Jesus are those beheaded for testifying about Jesus and the WORD of GOD and those who did not receive the mark of the beast.)
>
> (Matthew 19:28-30; Luke 22:24-30; Revelation 20:4-6)
>
> (Note: Oral church tradition has long assumed these twelve thrones belong to the twelve named disciples in the New Testament who walked with Yeshua/Jesus. That scenario would include Judas Iscariot, who many say was the betrayer of Jesus and others believe was Jesus' friend. An alternative interpretation is presented in the Gospel of Matthew, which says the good news promises in the Bible apply to any one who believes, and that it's Jesus who decides who

has actually followed Him—see Matthew 9:27-29, 21:21-22, 25:31-46; John 14:1, 6-7; Hebrews 11:6)

Twenty-four Thrones

> Twenty-four thrones surround the heavenly throne, on which sit twenty-four elders dressed in white robes with crowns of gold on their heads. Whenever the four living creatures praise and give glory to the LORD GOD ALMIGHTY, the twenty-four elders fall down to worship the One seated on the Throne. Who occupies the twenty-four thrones is unknown. Revelation 14:1-3 indicates the elders do not come from among the 144,000 redeemed from the Earth; 2. Members of the Amen Choir in heaven.
>
> (Revelation 4:1-4, 9-11, 5:6-14, 11;16-18, 20:4a; John 10:14-16)

Unclean/Unclean Spirit

> Soiled, impure, immoral, profane, forbidden and offensive.
>
> (Deuteronomy 14:1-21; 1 Samuel 20:26; Isaiah 6:5, 64:6; Jeremiah 2:22; Acts 10:28; 2 Corinthians 6:17; Revelation 16:13-14, 22:11)

Un-Forgiveness

> The unwillingness to give up one's right to get even; 2. Letting emotions (i.e. vengeance, anger, grief, pain, heartbreak) take the reins so that forgiveness is not allowed to enter in and abide.
>
> (Proverbs 24:17-18; Matthew 6:14-15, 18:21-35; Luke 6:37-38, 17:3-4; Romans 12:19; Colossians 3:12-14; 1 John 4:20)

Ungodly

> The evil, wicked and unrighteous; 2. One who consciously refuses to recognize, acknowledge or submit to GOD's authority.
>
> (Psalm 1:5-6; Isaiah 57:20-21; Daniel 12:10; Zephaniah 3:6-7; 1 Corinthians 6:9-10; 1 Timothy 1:8-10; 1 Peter 4:18; 2 Peter 2:1-19)

Vessels of Wrath and **V**essels of Mercy

> Vessels of wrath—those prepared beforehand (before the foundation of the Earth) as servants for destruction. Vessels of mercy—those prepared beforehand for GOD's glory.

(Luke 11:29-37; Romans 9:22-23; Revelation 14:9-11)

Vision

Special sight given by GOD for the purpose of revealing or exposing information and increasing the hearer's understanding; 2. Fantasies created in the minds of those who despise the WORD of the LORD; 3. The mental imagery of a future which does not yet exist.

(Numbers 12:6-8; Jeremiah 14:13-14, 23:16-18; Ezekiel 22:28; Daniel 7:13-14; Habakkuk 2:2-3; Amos 4-9; Zechariah 3:1-10; Matthew 7:15-20; Mark 13:21-23; Luke 3:21-22; Acts 9:10-12, 16:9-10: Revelation 1:1-2, 19:11-21, 21:1-27, 22:1-5)

Watcher

An angel or celestial being responsible for watching rulers of the world, reporting the degree to which they are fulfilling GOD's plans, and issuing decrees and verdicts according to the Most High GOD; 2. To be awake, or the watchful one.

(Ezekiel 33:1-7; Daniel 4:13, 17, 23)

Watchman/Watchwoman

The designation given to slaves or servants of GOD responsible for watching for danger and relaying warnings from GOD to the people, wicked and righteous alike; 2. A preacher; 3. A guardian.

(Psalm 130:6; Song of Solomon 3:3; Isaiah 21:6-12; Ezekiel 3:16-21, 33:1-11; Hosea 9:8)

Way (The)

A term once used to identify the followers of Yeshua/Jesus of Nazareth. Unclear is whether they named themselves or adversaries labeled them the "Way". In either case the designation aligns with Jesus who says in John 14, "I am the way, the truth, and the life"; 2. To travel in the same direction as another, according to the other person's preferences and desires.

(Psalm 119:1; Isaiah 35:8, 53:6, 57:14; Luke 18:18-22; John 14:1-6; Acts 8:1-3, 9:1-2, 18:24-25; 19:9, 23, 22:4-5, 24:14)

Weary

> The breaking point; 2. Exhausted and ready to give up; 3. Battle-fatigued.
>
> (Psalm 69:3, 73:26; Proverbs 3:11; Isaiah 40:28-31, 41:10, 50:4a; Jeremiah 31:25; Matthew 11:28-30; John 16:33; Galatians 6:9; Philippians 4:13; 2 Thessalonians 3:13; Hebrews 4:15-16, 12:3-4)

Wicked (see Ungodly)

Wilderness

> Experiencing a sensation of lack; 2. The feeling of being in the middle of nowhere and not recognizing anything.
>
> (Exodus 15:22; Isaiah 43:19; Ezekiel 34:25; Matthew 4:1; Mark 1:12-13; Revelation 12:5-6)

Will (GOD's)

> What GOD desires and commands.
>
> (Proverbs 3:5-6, 16:9, 19:21; Jeremiah 29:11; Micah 6:8; Matthew 6:10, 33; John 6:40, 7:17; Romans 8:28, 12:2; 1 Thessalonians 4:3-6, 5:16-22; James 1:5; 1 Peter 2:15; 2 Peter 3:9)

Witness

> One who remembers and can testify about a matter seen with their own eyes, heard with their own ears, or experienced firsthand; 2. To give evidence or bear testimony.
>
> (1 Kings 10:6-7; Psalm 66:16; Proverbs 12:17; Isaiah 6:8, 43:10-12; Mark 5:19-20; John 4:42, 5:39-40, 8:17-18; Acts 4:19-20, 5:30-32; 1 John 5:6-11; Revelation 12:11. Witnesses will often say "I looked...saw...heard...watched")

Witnesses (Two)

> Two anointed witnesses for GOD, who also stand with the Lord of the Earth, publicly prophecy for 1,260 days (42 months) dressed in sackcloth, as nations run roughshod over the saints and the holy city of Jerusalem. Anyone who attempts to harm them is consumed, and the two anointed ones are vested with power to prevent rain from

falling, to turn water to blood, and to inflict plagues as often as they desire. When their testimony is completed, the beast from the bottomless pit rises up and kills them. For three and a half days, their bodies lie in the street of the great city. The dwellers of the Earth rejoice and celebrate that the two witnesses tormenting them with their testimonies are dead. Some among the peoples, tribes, languages and nations (who know what the prophecy says) refuse to allow Earth dwellers to bury the bodies. After three and a half days, a breath from GOD enters them and they stand up, provoking great fear among those who see it happen. As their enemies watch, the witnesses are taken up to heaven in a cloud and in that same hour a great earthquake occurs, killing seven thousand people. Those belonging to the peoples, tribes, languages and nations are terrified and give glory to the GOD of heaven (unlike those of the Earth who do not repent of their sins, i.e. Revelation 9:6, 20-21, 16:9-11, 21). This concludes the passing of the second of three woes. Next comes the blowing of the seventh trumpet.

(Revelation 11:1-14, 14:8, 17:5, 18, 18:2, 10, 21, 20:1-3; Genesis 8:11; Jeremiah 2:21, 11:16-17; Zechariah 4:1-14; Matthew 5:14-16; James 5:17-18)

Woe

Torment, misery, distress, anguish, pain, despair, grief, suffering, agony, disasters, tribulations, and hardship.

(Job 10: 15; Ecclesiastes 10:16; Isaiah 3:11, 5:20-25, 45:9-14; Jeremiah 10:19, 23:1-4; Habakkuk 2:12; Matthew 23:23; Luke 6:24-26, 11:52, 22:22)

- First Woe (Revelation 9:1-12)
- Second Woe (Revelation 11:1-14)
- Third Woe (Revelation 12:7-12)

Woke

To be conscious and awake; 2. A state of alertness and focus.

(Proverbs 6:9; Isaiah 52:1-2; Matthew 24:42; Mark 4:38-39; Luke 12:40, 21:34-36; Romans 13:11-12; 1 Corinthians 16:13; Ephesians 5:13-14, 6:16-18; Colossians 4:2; 1 Thessalonians 4:13-18, 5:5-6; Revelation 3:2-3, 16:15)

Woman

One half of the human race created by the WORD in the image of GOD; 2. Helper, or *ezer*, to the Man (i.e. Psalm 46:1: "GOD is...a very present help (*ezer*) in trouble." The term <u>helper</u> has traditionally been translated and viewed as a subordinate position (i.e. the Woman is inferior, or under, the Man), but this interpretation is not easily supported by the biblical text; 2. The first witness to see and deliver the news about the resurrection of Yeshua/Jesus; 3. Regarded in heaven as divine; 4. A study published in 1987, "Mitochondrial DNA and Human Evolution," investigated the family tree of human evolution. The study's conclusion was that all human beings come from a single Woman, nicknamed "Mitochondrial Eve."

(Genesis 1:26-30, 2:5-8, 18-22, 3:8-16; 5:1-32, 6:1-14; Deuteronomy 4:19; Jeremiah 31:22b; Matthew 28:1-10; Mark 16:1-8; Luke 1:26-30, 24:1-11; John 1:1-4, 20:11-18; Revelation 12:1-6, 13-17)

- In the first creation story, both the woman and man are created simultaneously, both stand together before GOD, and both receive the same charges and list of responsibilities (Genesis 1:26-30).
- In the second creation story GOD first creates a man, decides it's not good for the man to be alone, and a woman is birthed out of the man's body (Genesis 2:5-23).
- In the third creation story, on the day GOD creates humankind in the image of the Creator, GOD (i.e. "GOD said...") is ascribed a masculine (male/Adam) form and introduced by the pronoun <u>he</u> (i.e. "He said..."). The lack of a definite article prior to the word Adam suggests a proper noun—a name—rather than a title. This is chilling, given that when Moses asked GOD for a name to give to the people, GOD answered Moses, "I AM WHO I AM. Tell them, I AM has sent you to them." Moving forward in the Bible, the voice and presence of the Woman is diminished or silenced altogether (Genesis 5:1-2; Exodus 3:10-12)
- When men began multiplying on the earth, they begin taking multiple women as wives. When GOD sees how great the wickedness of man is on the earth, the decision is made to destroy all men because the earth is filled with

such violence through them. Only a man named Noah finds favor in the eyes of GOD (Genesis 6:1-8).

Woman (The) and the Dragon

John sees a great sign in heaven, shown to him as an image of a woman clothed with the sun, a moon under her feet, and a crown of twelve stars on her head. She is pregnant and crying out in agony from labor pains and giving birth. A second sign appears in the form of a great red dragon having seven heads, ten horns, and a crown on each of its seven heads. His tail violently sweeps a third of the stars in heaven down to the Earth. The dragon stands before the woman, ready to destroy the child the moment it is born, but the child is caught up to GOD. The woman flies off into the wilderness to a placed prepared for her by GOD, where she is sustained for 1,260 days (forty-two months). Defeated, the dragon goes on to make war with the rest of her offspring, those who keep the commandments of GOD and hold fast to the testimony of Jesus.

(Revelation 12:1-6, 17; Genesis 3:12-16; Isaiah 66:7-14; Matthew 2:13-23)

WORD

GOD, and the word-of-mouth expression of GOD's thoughts and will; 2. Yeshua/Jesus of Nazareth, the WORD made flesh; 3. The Spirit through whom all things are created and all good things come; 4. The sword of the spirit; 5. Wisdom, knowledge and understanding given for the benefit of the hearer; 6. "The moral activity against which evil men break themselves." (Walter Brueggerman).

(Genesis 1 ("GOD said…"); John 1:1-5,14, 4:24,15:3, 26; Exodus 4:21-23, 5:1; Proverbs 2:1-5, 4:20, 30:5-6; Isaiah 55:10-11, 59:21; Jeremiah 30:18, 31:1, 32:6; Ezekiel 12:1,8, 17, 28:25 ("This says the Lord…"); Matthew 7:24-27, 24:35; Luke 11:27-28; Ephesians 6:17; 1 Thessalonians 2:13; 2 Timothy 3:16-17; Hebrews 4:12-13; James 1:19-22; Revelation 1:1-2,19:9)

Works (Good)

The offspring or behavior of faith and good conduct; 2. To labor, act on, do, or keep the WORD in truth; 3. Righteousness in action.

(Nehemiah 13:14; Psalm 90:17; Proverbs 3:6, 27; Isaiah 5:11-12; Matthew 5:14-16, 6:1-4, 19:16-17; John 3:20-21, 6:28-29, 10:32; Acts 10:37-38; 1 Corinthians 3:12-15; 2 Corinthians 5:10; Galatians 5:6; Colossians 1:9-10; 1 Timothy 5:9-10; 2 Timothy 3:16-17; Titus 3:8,14; Hebrews 6:10-12, 10:24; James 1:22-25, 2:14-20, 24-26; 1 John 3:17-18: Revelation 14:13, 20:12-13)

Xenophobia

A severe dislike, fear or hatred of the 'other'. Elements of xenophobia include: colonization, apartheid, antisemitism, racism, segregation, bigotry, discrimination, religious discrimination, sexism, prejudice, bias, anti-multiculturalism, blind patriotism and narrow-mindedness.

(Genesis 4:3-8; Deuteronomy 23:1-6; Nehemiah 2:17-20, 4:1-3, 7-8; Luke 4:16, 22, 28-29; Acts 7:51-58, 9:1, 22-25, 11:1-4, 18, 12:1-3, 14:1-2, 19; 15:1, 36-40; 19:23-34)

Yeshua

The name means 'Yahweh saves', or 'Yahweh is salvation'. The English spelling of Yeshua is Joshua (Gr. Iēsous) and the English transcription of Iēsous is Jesus, meaning to save, rescue or deliver; 2. The name of the firstborn Son of Mary; 3. The name is associated with Levitical priests (i.e. *Jeshua* mentioned in the Hebrew Bible); 4. The Prince of princes and Prince of the heavenly hosts; 5. The Lion of the tribe of Judah; 6. The Lamb that was slain, having seven horns and seven eyes, the seven spirits of GOD.

(1 Chronicles 24:11; 2 Chronicles 31:15; Ezra 3:2, 4:3, 5:2, etc.; Nehemiah 3:19, 7:7, 8:7, etc.; Daniel 8:11, 25b; Luke 1:30-32; Revelation 5:5-6)

Youth

The season of childhood innocence, fantasies, foolishness, vanity and indiscretions; 2. A mind attentive to matters of the flesh, rather than the spirit.

(Judges 14:1-2, 16:1, 4; Psalm 25:7, 119:9; Proverbs 20:11; Ecclesiastes 11:9-10, 12:1; Isaiah 40:30-31; Jeremiah 1:4-8; Lamentations 3:27; 1 Corinthians 3:1-3, 13:11; Ephesians 4:11-14; 1Timothy 4:12; 2 Timothy 2:22)

Zeal/Zealous

> An intense or tireless devotion toward a person, or on behalf of a movement or belief.
>
> (2 Samuel 21:2; 2 Kings 10:15-17; Isaiah 37:30-32; John 2:13-17, 4:34, Romans 10:1-4; 2 Corinthians 7:10-11; Revelation 2:4-5, 13, 3:8)

Zion

> Symbolizing: 1. GOD's Holy mountain or hill of everlasting joy; 2. The mountain height of Israel; 3. The people of GOD; 4. The City of the Lord; 5. Virgin Israel; 6. The Bride and wife of the Lamb; 7. The new Jerusalem.
>
> (Psalm 2:1-6; Isaiah 35:10; 51:3, 16, 60:14; Jeremiah 31:1-6; Ezekiel 20:40; Obadiah 1:17; John 1:14-18, 10:16; Hebrews 12:18-24; 1 Peter 2:4-6; Revelation 14:1, 21:1-2, 9-27)

www.ingramcontent.com/pod-product-compliance
Lightning Source LLC
Chambersburg PA
CBHW020556030426
42337CB00013B/1114